AIR CAMPAIGN

SINKING FORCE Z 1941

The day the Imperial Japanese Navy killed the battleship

ANGUS KONSTAM | ILLUSTRATED BY ADAM TOOBY

OSPREY PUBLISHING
Bloomsbury Publishing Plc
PO Box 883, Oxford, OX1 9PL, UK
1385 Broadway, 5th Floor, New York, NY 10018, USA
E-mail: info@ospreypublishing.com
www.ospreypublishing.com

OSPREY is a trademark of Osprey Publishing Ltd

First published in Great Britain in 2021

A catalogue record for this book is available from the British Library.

ISBN: PB 9781472846600; eBook 9781472846617;
ePDF 9781472846587; XML 9781472846594

21 22 23 24 25 10 9 8 7 6 5 4 3 2 1
Maps by www.bounford.com
Battlescenes and diagrams by Adam Tooby
3D BEVs by Paul Kime
Index by Alan Rutter
Typeset by PDQ Digital Media Solutions, Bungay, UK
Printed and bound in India by Replika Press Private Ltd.

Osprey Publishing supports the Woodland Trust, the UK's leading woodland conservation charity.

To find out more about our authors and books visit www.ospreypublishing.com. Here you will find extracts, author interviews, details of forthcoming events and the option to sign up for our newsletter.

Photographs

All photos in this book are courtesy of the Stratford Archive.

Note

Where the term "mile" is used, unless noted otherwise this refers to a nautical mile as defined by both Britain and Japan in 1941. This was 6,080 feet long (2,026 ⅔ yards), the equivalent of 1,853m or 1.85km. By contrast a British land mile in 1941 was 5,280 feet long, equating to 1,760 yards (1,609m, or 1.61km). To confuse things slightly, at the time, for the purposes of gunnery the British also used "sea miles", with which were 2,000 yards (1,829m) long.

CONTENTS

INTRODUCTION

The elderly battlecruiser *Repulse* first saw action during World War I, and although she had been extensively modernised during the 1930s, she still lacked sufficient anti-aircraft firepower to adequately defend herself against a large-scale air attack.

On Wednesday 10 December 1941, a powerful British battlegroup was at sea in the Gulf of Siam. It was three days since the Japanese attack on Pearl Harbor. By late morning it was 43 nautical miles off the eastern coast of the Malay Peninsula. The force had sortied from Singapore two days before, in an attempt to disrupt Japanese amphibious landings on the Malay Peninsula. Now, Force Z – the battleship *Prince of Wales*, the battlecruiser *Repulse* and three destroyers – were heading east, away from the coast, as the operation had been called off. Away to the north, lookouts spotted an aircraft, a Japanese scout plane. Although it

Prime Minister Winston Churchill (1874–1965) and Admiral Sir Tom Phillips (1888–1941), pictured outside the Admiralty building in Whitehall in early 1941. Both men were instrumental in the decision to send Force Z to the Far East, regardless of the potential threat posed by Japanese land-based air power in South-East Asia.

The King George V-class battleship *Prince of Wales* had seen action before, in May 1941, when she engaged the German battleship *Bismarck* in the battle of the Denmark Strait. Now she was being sent into harm's way again, and would fight another battle she was equally ill-prepared for.

quickly disappeared, on board the battleship Admiral Phillips was under no illusions. Force Z had been sighted, and that meant an air attack was imminent. At that moment, due to a series of misunderstandings, Force Z had no air cover and as they lacked modern anti-aircraft defences; the two capital ships were vulnerable. Sure enough, less than an hour later, the Japanese returned in force.

They came at 1140hrs. In the first attack, the *Prince of Wales* was hit by a torpedo, causing flooding and a drop in speed and power. She was still limping along 40 minutes later when the next wave appeared. This time she was hit by three more torpedoes, while *Repulse* was also hit at least five times. These were mortal blows. The *Prince of Wales* sank an hour after this second attack, after *Repulse* had already gone to the bottom. A total of 840 of their crew went down with them. That day, the Royal Navy's offensive power in the Far East was obliterated. With the Americans still reeling from Pearl Harbor, and the Japanese army advancing rapidly towards Singapore, a horrified Churchill realised that, as he put it, 'Japan was supreme, and we everywhere were weak and naked.' The repercussions were immense. Stripped of its naval protection, the fate of Singapore was sealed. The Commonwealth garrison there surrendered in mid-February 1942. It was a blow from which British military prestige in the Far East would never recover.

Above all, the sinking of Force Z exposed the fallacy that sea power rested on the big gun, rather than the aircraft. For over half a century, the battleship had dominated naval warfare but, during the inter-war years and for those willing to heed the signs, this supremacy was challenged by the growing efficiency of naval air power. In the opening years of the war, the vulnerability of the Royal Navy's surface warships to attack from the air was demonstrated off Norway, Dunkirk and Crete. Despite this, the British Admiralty sent Force Z to bolster Britain's naval presence in the Far East. These two capital ships were sent to Singapore to act as a deterrent. Instead, it was thrust into the forefront of a naval campaign for which it was poorly equipped. With a Japanese invasion of Malaya imminent, Force Z was sent to intercept the enemy landing force, but was ambushed by land-based aircraft, and overwhelmed.

The naval implications of this debacle were profound. It offered clear proof that the battleship was little more than a liability in a modern naval war. In December 1941, though, even the Japanese placed an undue emphasis on the offensive power of the battleship. At the time the British Admiralty never questioned the value of sending Force Z to sea to seek out the enemy. That all changed that day, in the Gulf of Siam. From that point on, naval air power reigned supreme. The disaster signalled the end of the battleship as an offensive weapon, except under very limited or exceptional circumstances. They were just too vulnerable to put in harm's way. It was a lesson the British eventually took on board, but it was one learned at a terrible cost, in men, ships and national standing. The sinking of Force Z was arguably Britain's greatest naval disaster of World War II. The aim of this book is to show just how and why this calamity happened.

CHRONOLOGY

1941

28 August Battlecruiser *Repulse* ordered to sail for Far East, as a convoy escort.

20 October War Cabinet's Defence Committee decides to send naval reinforcements to Singapore.

23 October Battleship *Prince of Wales* sails from Scapa Flow, bound for Far East.

25 October After embarking Admiral Phillips and staff, *Prince of Wales* sails from the Clyde.

3 November Aircraft carrier *Indomitable* runs aground off Bermuda.

5 November *Prince of Wales* puts in to Freetown, Sierra Leone.

16–18 November *Prince of Wales* puts in to Cape Town, South Africa.

28 November *Prince of Wales* reaches Colombo, Ceylon (now Sri Lanka), and joins *Repulse*.

29 November Foundering of diplomatic negotiations between Japan and United States.

2 December Force Z arrives in Singapore.

Monday 8 December

0045hrs Japanese commence landing operations on coast of Siam and northern Malaya. Britain and Commonwealth now at war with Japan.

1230hrs Admiral Phillips holds an operational briefing on board *Prince of Wales.*

1710hrs Force Z leaves Singapore.

Tuesday 9 December

0713hrs Force Z passes point to east of Anamba Islands, and turns northwards.

1415hrs British naval force sighted by Japanese submarine I-65.

1645hrs Weather improves, and skies clear.

1650hrs Japanese search planes take off from bases in Indochina.

1730hrs Japanese naval air strike takes off from Saigon.

1745hrs Force Z sighted by Japanese float plane.

1809hrs Sunset.

1850hrs Japanese bombers accidentally attack the Japanese heavy cruiser *Chokai.*

1856hrs *Chokai* sets off a flare, seen by British destroyer.

1858hrs Force Z and Japanese Covering Force alter course and head away from each other without detecting one another.

2050hrs Admiral Phillips cancels attack on Japanese transport force off Singora.

2352hrs Message from Singapore informs Palliser of Japanese landings taking place at Kuantan.

Force Z spotted by Japanese submarine I-58. Subsequent torpedo attack fails.

Wednesday 10 December

0010hrs Admiral Phillips decides to redirect Force Z towards Kuantan, to oppose Japanese landings.

0211hrs Sighting report by I-58 reaches Rear-Admiral Matsunaga's headquarters in Saigon.

0315hrs I-58 loses contact with Force Z.

0500hrs Nine Japanese reconnaissance planes take off from Saigon.

0503hrs Dawn.

0515hrs Force Z spots Japanese tug and barges during approach to Kuantan.

0625hrs Genzan *Kokutai* takes off from Saigon.

0644hrs Kanoya *Kokutai* takes off from Dau Mot.

0650hrs Mihoro *Kokutai* begins taking off from Dau Mot.

0738hrs Walrus float plane conducts air reconnaissance of Kuantan – reports no Japanese landings there.

0900hrs Destroyer *Express* returns from reconnaissance of Kuantan, and confirms no landings are taking place there.

0930hrs Force Z turns away from coast, and heads towards south-east.

1005hrs Destroyer *Tenedos* (RAN) sighted by Japanese search plane, and attacked.

1015hrs *Tenedos* bombed by squadron of Genzan *Kokutai*, but emerges unscathed.

Force Z sighted by Japanese reconnaissance aircraft.

1040hrs Force Z detects approaching bomber formations on radar.

1109hrs Force Z opens fire.

1113hrs 1 Sqn/Mihoro conducts bombing attack on *Repulse*. Battlecruiser hit by a 250kg bomb.

1141hrs 1 Sqn/Genzan conducts torpedo attack on *Prince of Wales*.

1144hrs *Prince of Wales* hit by torpedo on port side aft. Damages port outer propeller shaft.

1149hrs 2 Sqn/Genzan attacks *Repulse*, but battlecruiser evades all torpedoes.

1150hrs *Prince of Wales* now crippled, and listing heavily to port.

1157hrs 1 Sqn/Mihoro returns to conduct second attack on *Repulse*. No hits.

1158hrs Ceasefire.

1204hrs Captain Tennant of *Repulse* contacts Singapore, and requests air support.

1210hrs *Prince of Wales* hoists 'Not under Control' signal – steering erratically.

1220hrs Admiral Phillips breaks radio silence, and contacts Singapore.

Fresh wave of aircraft spotted to east, moving in to attack.

1221hrs Force Z opens fire on approaching aircraft.

1223hrs Elements of Kanoya attack *Prince of Wales*. Battleship hit three times on starboard side.

1224hrs Elements of Kanoya attack *Repulse* from multiple directions. Battlecruiser hit by torpedo on port side aft.

1225hrs *Repulse* struck by four more torpedoes – battlecruiser left crippled and sinking. Order given to abandon ship.

1230hrs Air attack ends.

1232hrs *Repulse* sinks.

1240hrs Final wave of Japanese bombers appear.

1241hrs 2 Sqn and 3 Sqn/Mihoro attack *Prince of Wales*.

1244hrs *Prince of Wales* hit by 500kg bomb. Extensive casualties amidships.

1250hrs Captain Leach of *Prince of Wales* requests tugs sent from Singapore to tow battleship home.

1300hrs Evacuation of non-essential crew from battleship, including engine room staff.

1310hrs Order given to abandon ship. Destroyer *Express* used as rescue vessel.

1315hrs *Prince of Wales* begins to capsize – *Express* damaged and forced to break free of sinking battleship.

1320hrs Fighter cover from No. 453 Squadron arrives over remains of Force Z.

1323hrs *Prince of Wales* sinks.

Before the outbreak of war in the Pacific, the British knew very little about the potential of Japanese land-based aircraft, and greatly underestimated the threat they posed to British naval power in the region. In fact, Japanese aircraft like this Type 96 bomber were much more advanced than Western intelligence analysts had anticipated.

ATTACKER'S CAPABILITIES

The new rulers of the sea

A Japanese naval *Kokutai* (Air Corps) consisted of three or more squadrons, each of up to nine aircraft. In the attacks on Force Z in December 1941, three of these *Kokutai* were deployed in the hunt for the British warships.

Air assets

In September 1940, the Japanese entered French Indochina after reaching an agreement with the Vichy French government. While Japanese troops occupied the French colony, the Imperial Japanese Navy were able to use French naval facilities, and the large protected anchorage of Cam Ranh Bay. The Army Air Force moved air units into the country, but initially these were dedicated to the support of land-based forces. So, with a view to supporting the ambitious operations planned by the Imperial Japanese Navy in the region, its Commander-in-Chief, Admiral Yamamoto decided to redeploy its own aircraft there. In November the 22nd *Koku Sentai* (Air Flotilla) was ordered to relocate from the Chinese island of Formosa to new bases in southern Indochina. The formation would take over former French airfields near Saigon, and prepare itself for active operations beginning 8 December 1941 (7 December to the east of the International Date Line).

The 22nd Air Flotilla was commanded by Rear-Admiral Sadaichi Matsunaga (1892–1965), a highly experienced officer who had taken command of the air formation that January. His command consisted of two *Kokutai* (Air Groups, or Air Corps), each consisting of three or four bomber squadrons. The Genzan *Kokutai*, named after its original base, consisted of 36 Mitsubishi Navy Type 96 G3M2 two-engined bombers (codenamed 'Nell' by the Allies). The second formation was the Mihoro *Kokutai*, which had the same strength and aircraft type. However, shortly before the campaign began, and following news that Force Z was due to arrive in Singapore, Yamamoto decided to reinforce the air flotilla. As such, the veteran Kanoya *Kokutai* was detached from the 21st *Kokutai*, based in Formosa, and sent to Saigon. It consisted of 27 Mitsubishi Navy Type 1 G4M1 'Betty' two-engined bombers.

This gave Matsunaga a total of 99 bombers, all capable of carrying either torpedoes or conventional bombs. These were supported by the Yamada Air Unit, with 36 fighters and six dedicated reconnaissance aircraft: a mixture of 11 Mitsubishi A4M 'Claude' and 24 Mitsubishi A6M 'Zero' single-seater fighters, and six Mitsubishi C5M 'Babs' two-seater reconnaissance planes. These were all based at Soc Trang to the south of Saigon in the Mekong Delta, but would take no part in the attack on Force Z due to their lack of range. Instead, Matsunaga would rely on his bombers for both reconnaissance and bombing missions.

Mitsubishi Type 96 G3M2 'Nell'	
Crew:	Seven (six during attack on Force Z)
Length:	16.45m (54ft)
Wingspan:	25m (82ft)
Weight (fully laden):	8,000kg (17,637lb)
Engines:	Two Mitsubishi Kinsei piston engines
Speed:	Maximum: 202 knots Cruising: 150 knots
Ceiling:	9,200m (30,184ft)
Climb rate:	6m (19.7ft) per second
Range:	2,400 nautical miles
Armament:	One 20mm machine gun (MG) in upper turret, four 7.7mm MGs facing forward
Payload:	One aerial torpedo, or up to 800kg of bombs
Entered service:	1935

The Mihoro *Kokutai* was based to the north of the city, at Dau Mot. The remainder were based in Saigon itself, at the former civilian aerodrome of Tan Son Nhut. This was also the location of Matsunaga's headquarters, with its intelligence and communication sections. By redeploying the Kanoya *Kokutai*, Yamamoto had weakened the air units supporting the impending attack on the Philippines. Still, the admiral considered the threat posed by Force Z warranted this last-minute redeployment. It also provided Matsunaga with his most modern bombers, and his best-trained air crews. Their Type 1 G4M1 was known as the *Hamaki* ('cigar') by its crews, due to its cigar-like shape. It lacked armoured protection for its six-man crew, or self-sealing fuel tanks, so the Allies eventually labelled it 'The Type 1 Lighter'. Nevertheless, with a range of just over 1,500 nautical miles, and a cruising speed of 170 knots, it was able to range far out to sea in search of enemy vessels, and could carry a single Type 91 aerial torpedo, or either a 500kg or 800kg bomb. The aircraft first entered active service in 1940.

The Type 96 bomber, however, was essentially the forerunner of the Type 1. It also had a six-man crew, although both aircraft were later supplied with more guns and an extra gunner. It entered service in 1937, and proved its worth during Japanese operations in China. The Type 96 had a similar range, speed and payload to the Type 1, and it too lacked the armoured protection and self-sealing tanks that were becoming standard in other air forces during this period. This bomber was well-armed, though, and like the Type 1, it was extremely versatile. It was capable of performing high-level bombing missions or low-level torpedo attacks with equal aplomb, and had the range Matsunaga needed to attack Force Z anywhere in the Gulf of Siam, if it came within his reach. To this end the Type 96, with its bubble-shaped front canopy, made a useful long-range search aircraft. The air crews of the flotilla were therefore as well versed in long-range search techniques as they were in using their bombs or torpedoes.

Admiral of the Fleet Isoroko Yamamoto (1884–1943) was the leading architect of Japan's ambitious war plans. Thanks to his efforts, in early December 1941 Japan was poised to strike a devastating blow against American and British forces in the Pacific. His advocacy of naval air power led directly to the creation of a powerful force of land-based naval aircraft.

Japanese army airfields
Japanese navy airfields
Japanese invasion route
Japanese minefield
Landing beaches
SIAM
Bangkok
BURMA
INDOCHINA
Gulf of Siam
XXXX
Tomoyuki
Cam Ran
Bay
Dau Mot
Saigon (Tan Son Nhut)
Kompong Trach
Duong Dong
Convoy
Splits
Cape
Cambodia
Singora
Patani
Alor Star
Kota Bharu
Sungei Patani
Gong Kedak
Butterworth
Panang Island
MALAYA
Malacca Strait
XXX
III Ind
Percival
Kuantan
NATUNA
ISLANDS
ANAMBA
ISLANDS
Kuala Lumpur
Tioman
Sumatra
Kluang
N
Singapore
Singapore Strait
0
100 miles
0
100km
Borneo

OPPOSITE THE STRATEGIC SITUATION, SOUTH-EAST ASIA, DECEMBER 1941

Mitsubishi Type 1 G4M1 'Betty'	
Crew:	Seven (six during attack on Force Z)
Length:	19.97m (65ft 6in)
Wingspan:	24.89m (81ft 8in)
Weight (fully laden):	9,500kg (20,944lb)
Engines:	Two Mitsubishi Kinsei piston engines
Speed:	Maximum: 231 knots Cruising: 170 knots
Ceiling:	9,100m (29,855ft)
Climb rate:	9.2m (30.2ft) per second
Range:	1,540 nautical miles
Armament:	One 20mm machine gun (MG) in rear turret, four 7.7mm MGs facing forward
Payload:	One aerial torpedo, or up to 858kg of bombs
Entered service:	1941

Of these two types of attack, high-level bombing was arguably the least effective. At this time, the Japanese had a limited stock of armour-piercing bombs, and these were earmarked for the Pearl Harbor operation. The 22nd Air Flotilla therefore had to use the 500kg (1,080lb) Type 50 Model 2 ordinary bomb, though its teardrop shape did give it a limited armour-piercing capability. If it hit a target – even a capital ship – it could be expected to plunge through any deck armour to explode in more vulnerable compartments beneath. Due to limited

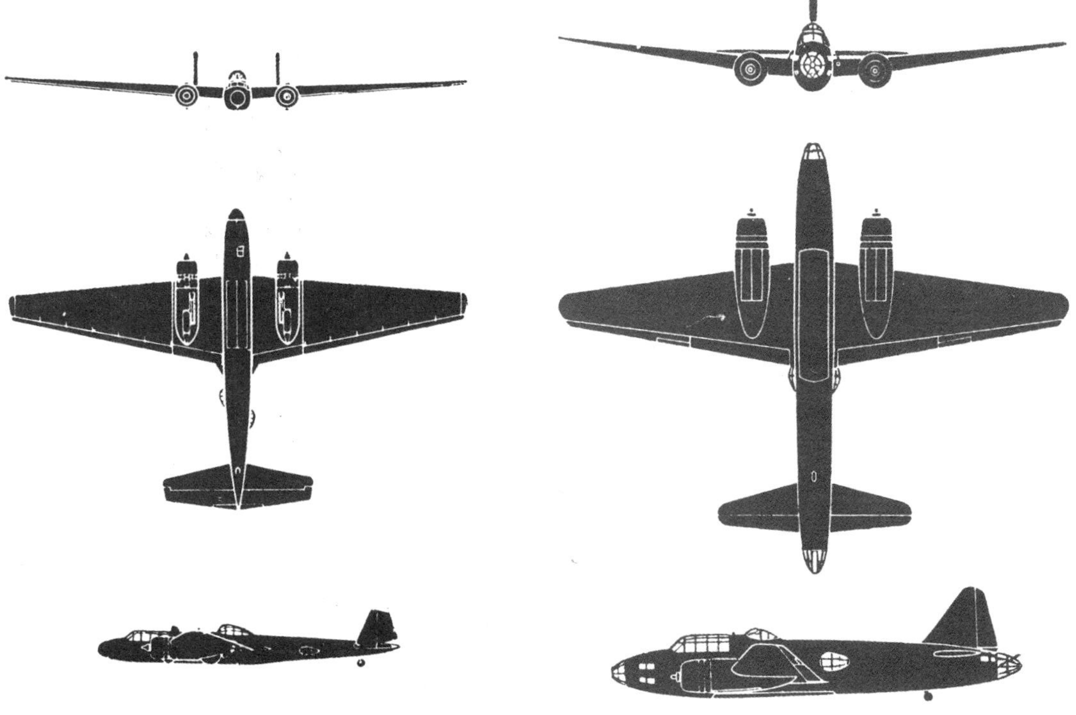

BELOW LEFT
The cornerstone of the Imperial Japanese Navy's land-based bomber force was the Mitsubishi Type 96 G3M. This twin-engined bomber, codenamed 'Nell' by the Allies, and depicted here in an American aircraft recognition card, could be deployed either as a conventional bomber or in a torpedo attack role.

BELOW RIGHT
The Mitsubishi Type 1 G4M was designed as the successor to the G3M, but in late 1941 both aircraft were still in widespread use. Its substantial range and effective payload made it perfect for the long-range projection of land-based naval air power in the Pacific.

A Type 1 bomber, accompanied at a distance by the rest of its squadron. In December 1941, these aircraft could either carry a single 500kg bomb, or an aerial torpedo. Switching the payload from one to the other was time-consuming, as it meant removing the bomb-bay doors if a torpedo was to be carried.

stocks of these, however, one squadron of the air flotilla would carry the smaller 250kg (557lb) Type 25 Model 2 ordinary bomb – two in each aircraft. These were of a similar shape to their larger counterparts, and so had a limited penetrative capability. The problem, though, was that high-level attacks needed to be pressed home in tight formations, to ensure a high probability of scoring a hit. This in turn made the bombers vulnerable to enemy fire.

An altogether superior weapon was the Type 91 Mod 1 aerial torpedo. Like most aerial torpedoes of this period it had a diameter of roughly 18in – in this case 45cm (17.7in), and was carried slung beneath the bombing aircraft. It could be released at speeds of up to 150 knots, and at heights of up to 35m (115ft). It was activated when it hit the water, and once it bobbed back up to its set depth – usually between 2 and 6 metres (6.5-20ft) – it ran at a speed of approximately 42 knots. It was fuelled by mixing kerosene and compressed air to produce a gas, which in turn powered the torpedo's small piston engine. This was a 'wet heater' design, where water was used to cool the machinery as it ran. The torpedo had a range of 2,000m (2,200 yards), and if it hit its target the explosive head containing 150kg (331lb) of high explosive would be detonated. The Kanoya *Kokutai* used a more modern Mod 2 version, which carried a slightly larger warhead of 205kg (452lb).

The secret with any torpedo attack was to 'lead' the target – aiming at a point where the tracks of the ship and the torpedo would intersect. Clearly a ship's captain would try to avoid any approaching torpedoes by turning his ship to 'comb' their tracks. Experienced torpedo bomber crews, however, could counter this by either leaving it until the last minute to drop their torpedo – for instance at a range of 600m (660 yards) or less – or to increase the chances of a hit by aircraft attacking the target simultaneously from different directions. During the attack on Force Z both of these techniques were employed, and proved highly successful. Still, it took nerve to fly a large two-engined bomber at low level, and maintain a steady course and speed until the torpedo was released. During these attacks, it was clear that some Japanese air crews were better

Japanese Naval Air Units, 10 December 1941

22nd Air Flotilla (Rear-Admiral Matsunaga). Based in Saigon.
Genzan *Kokutai* (Lieutenant-Commander Nakanishi)
Aircraft: Mitsubishi Type 96 G3M2 'Nell'
1st Squadron (Lieutenant Ishihara): 9 bombers (torpedoes)
2nd Squadron (Lieutenant Takai): 8 bombers (torpedoes)
3rd Squadron (Lieutenant Nikaido): 9 bombers (bombs)
Kanoya *Kokutai* (Lieutenant-Commander Miyauchi)
Aircraft: Mitsubishi Type 1 G4M1 'Betty'
1st Squadron (Lieutenant Nabeta): 9 bombers (torpedoes)
2nd Squadron (Lieutenant Higashimori): 8 bombers (torpedoes)
3rd Squadron (Lieutenant Iki): 9 bombers (torpedoes)
Mihoro *Kokutai* (under control of Lieutenant-Commander Nakanishi, Genzan *Kokutai*)
Aircraft: Mitsubishi Type 96 G3M2 'Nell'
1st Squadron (Lieutenant Shirai): 8 bombers (bombs)
2nd Squadron (Lieutenant Takeda): 8 bombers (bombs)
3rd Squadron (Lieutenant Ohira): 9 bombers (bombs)
4th Squadron (Lieutenant Takahashi): 8 bombers (torpedoes)
In addition, nine Mitsubishi Type 96 G3M2 'Nell' of the Genzan *Kokutai* operated as a reconnaissance force.

trained than others, and more willing to press home close-range attacks, to increase their chances of scoring a hit.

Naval and land assets

In early December 1941, the Imperial Japanese Navy was poised to launch a series of devastating attacks throughout the Pacific. The fleet would act as the spearhead of Japan's whirlwind expansion into the South and Central Pacific, South-East Asia and the East Indies. Therefore, while the country boasted a large and powerful fleet, these warships were committed to a range of operations, from the attack on Pearl Harbor to the invasion of the Philippines. In South-East Asia, the Army Minister General Tojo planned to invade Malaya by means of amphibious landings along the coast of southern Siam, followed by a rapid advance southwards through the Malay Peninsula. To protect the transport of the army, the Japanese Navy was expected to screen the transport ships, and prevent any British attempt to interfere with the landings.

The naval force assigned to screen these landings was commanded by Vice-Admiral Nobutake Kondo. He commanded the Japanese 2nd Fleet, which was based at Sanya on the Chinese island of Hainan. His fleet was really a scouting force, composed mainly of cruisers and destroyers. However, for this operation Kondo was given temporary control of a pair of battleships from the 1st Fleet. These formed the core of his Distant Cover Force, designed to support the amphibious landings in both the Philippines and Malaya by occupying a central position, and remaining ready to intervene in either operation if required. Their transfer was a direct result of the deployment of Force Z to the Far East and meant that his Distant Cover Force now consisted of the elderly battleships *Kongo* and *Haruna*, the heavy cruisers *Takao* and *Atago*, and nine destroyers.

These were to loiter close to Cambodia Point, the southernmost tip of Indochina. A second naval group, designated the Covering Force, under Vice-Admiral Jisaburo Ozawa with four heavy cruisers, one light cruiser and four destroyers would offer direct protection of the amphibious forces, and would be stationed between the landing beaches and Singapore. Finally, the amphibious attack forces themselves would be escorted by a small number of warships – two seaplane carriers, a light cruiser, ten destroyers and four minesweepers. The expectation was that if Force Z sortied from Singapore, the forces of Kondo and Ozawa would be able to intercept them, and keep them away from the transport ships.

FAR LEFT
Vice-Admiral Nobutake Kondo (1886–1953) was in command of the Japanese naval forces deployed in the Gulf of Siam during the Japanese invasion of Malaya. While he took no direct part in the air battle, his battleship force was crucial, as it was the only surface force with sufficient firepower to take on Force Z in a conventional naval battle.

LEFT
Vice-Admiral Jisaburo Ozawa (1886–1966) commanded the naval Covering Force charged with protecting the Japanese invasion fleet used in the landings in Siam and Malaya. At one point, in the night of 9–10 December, his force of cruisers and destroyers were minutes away from engaging Force Z in a night battle.

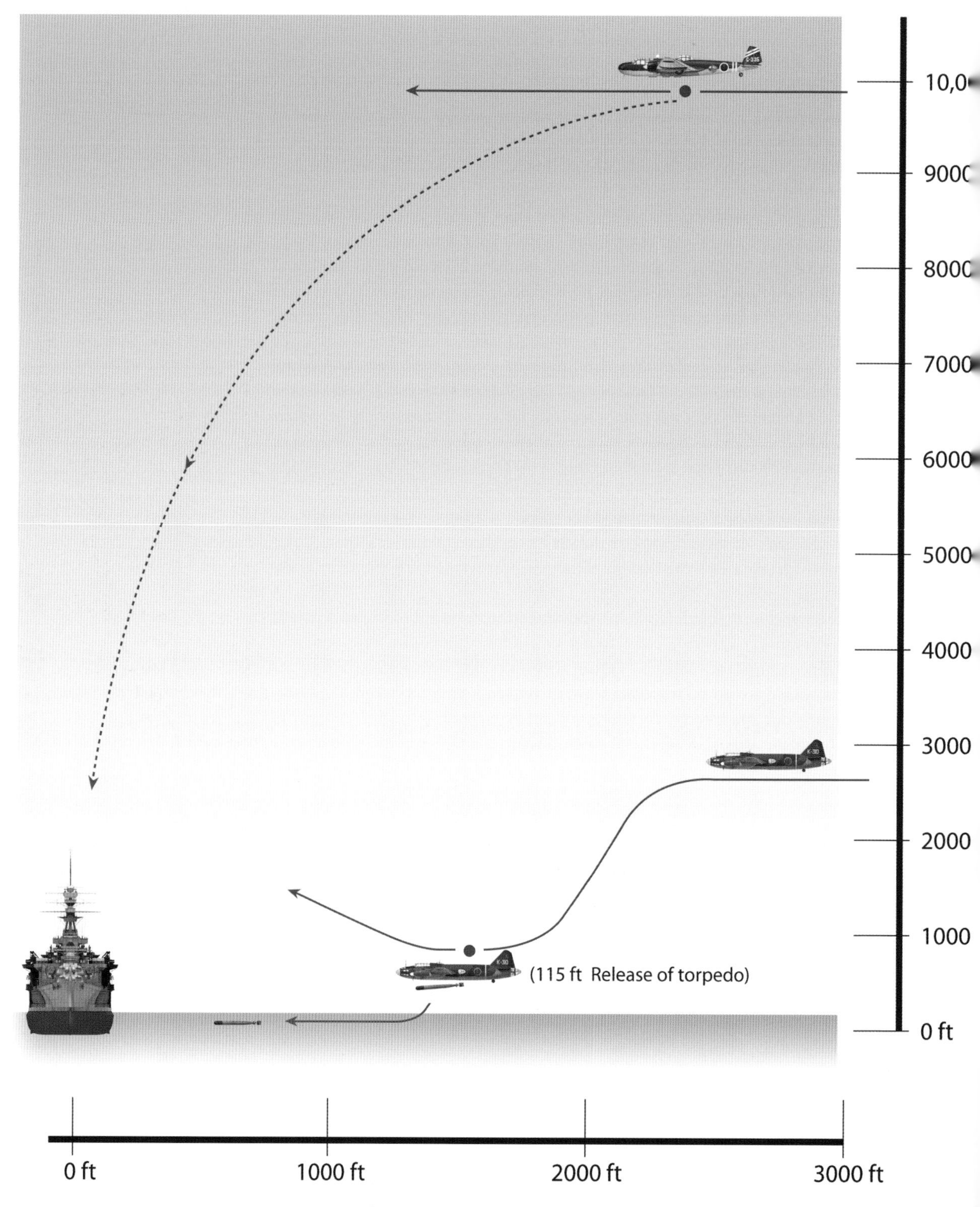
10,0
900
800
7000
6000
5000
4000
3000
2000
1000
0 ft
(115 ft Release of torpedo)
0 ft
1000 ft
2000 ft
3000 ft

OPPOSITE ATTACK TECHNIQUES EMPLOYED AGAINST FORCE Z

The Japanese bombers of the 22nd *Koku Sentai* (Air Flotilla) attacked the capital ships of Force Z in two ways, through high-level bombing and low-level torpedo attacks.

High-level bombing attack

Three of the nine attacking squadrons, comprising the 25 Type 96 G3M2 'Nell' bombers of the 1st–3rd squadrons, Mihoro *Kokutai* were armed with high explosive (HE) bombs.

1st Squadron (8 aircraft) – each carrying 2x 250kg HE bombs
2nd Squadron (8 aircraft) – each carrying 1x 500kg HE bomb
3rd Squadron (9 aircraft) – each carrying 1x 500kg HE bomb

Attacks were made at 3,000m, with air speeds of 120–150 knots. The approach was made in close formation as the aim was to saturate the target area, rather than allowing each bomber to achieve individual hits. Aiming was done by the squadron leader's aircraft, and the squadron released their bombs on his command. At that airspeed, the release point was approximately 800–1,000m ahead of the target. The aiming point was slightly ahead of the target ship, as the speed of the bombs' descent meant that the time of fall was just under 25 seconds. If we assume the *Repulse* was the target, making 26 knots, she could travel 334m in the fall time, the equivalent of two-thirds of her own length.

When the bomb struck, its terminal velocity of 242m per second was enough to punch its way through any lightly armoured deck, to explode in the compartment below. However, as these were HE bombs, they would be unable to penetrate the protective armoured deck below it, and thus there was no real chance of the bomb reaching the vitals of the ship – her magazines or propulsion spaces.

Low-level torpedo attack

The bombers of the remaining six squadrons of the 22nd *Koku Sentai* were armed with torpedoes – one per aircraft. When the target ship was sighted, these torpedo bombers would quickly drop down to a height of 1,000m, before continuing their descent during their approach to the target. The final approach before releasing the torpedo would be made while flying level at a height of 35m, at a speed of 150 knots.

These bombers carried a 45cm (17.7in) Type 91 torpedo – the Type 1 bombers of the Konoro *Kokutai* carried the Model 2 version, while the Type 96 aircraft of the remaining two groups carried the Model 1 version, which had a smaller warhead (150kg rather than 205kg). The torpedo had a maximum range of 2,000m, and a speed of approximately 42 knots. When released the torpedo would plunge up to 10m into the sea, before its hydrostatic controls steadied the torpedo at its running depth of 2–6 m. The normal release range from the minimum range to permit adequate arming time for the torpedo was 400m. Target was 750–1,000m, but during the attack several bombers released them at just over 500m.

Both battleships were of World War I vintage, dreadnoughts built to a British design; Kondo's flagship *Kongo* was actually built in Britain. They carried eight 14in guns, in four twin turrets, and so in terms of armament were a match for their two potential British opponents. These two Japanese battleships were extensively modernised during the 1930s and provided with modern fire control systems, search aircraft and a decent anti-aircraft capability. The Japanese heavy cruisers of Kondo and Ozawa's forces were each armed with ten 8in guns, which obviously lacked the penetrative power of the larger battleship guns. In a gunnery duel they would have been hard-pressed to achieve much against the two British capital ships.

However, all of these cruisers carried 24in 'Long Lance' torpedoes, which had a phenomenal range of up to 40,000m (43,700 yards) at 36 knots, or 20,000m (21,900 yards) at 48 knots. Ozawa's four heavy cruisers carried 56 of these – eight in the flagship and 12 in the rest. Even if we ignore the light cruiser *Kashi*, with its smaller and less effective 21in torpedoes, the four Fubuki-class destroyers under Ozawa's command carried another 36 'Long Lance' torpedoes between them. That meant that in any surface engagement against Force Z, the Japanese Covering Force and Distant Cover Force could launch up to 92 long-range torpedoes at the British ships, from a range that was beyond the enemy's effective range.

This, though, is a historical 'what might have been' as, during this campaign, a night-time clash between the two forces almost happened, but both sides broke contact at the

The Japanese heavy cruiser *Chokai* was Vice-Admiral Ozawa's flagship. When it was the subject of a potential 'friendly fire' bombing attack in the Gulf of Siam he ordered his ships to retire to the north, out of harm's way. At that moment, his Covering Force was just a few miles to the north of Force Z.

last minute. It might have been the case that there would have been no need to launch Rear-Admiral Matsunaga's bombers on 10 December after all, as Ozawa's torpedoes might already have done their job. Equally, it is also difficult to speculate what might have happened if Kondo's two capital ships had engaged their British counterparts in a more conventional gunnery duel. Even there, Kondo's nine destroyers also carried 'Long Lance' torpedoes, and so posed a serious threat to the British.

Kondo also had other assets to help him even the odds. First, two minelayers, the *Tatsumiya Maru* and the *Nagasa* would lay a minefield between the island of Tioman and the Anamba Islands, to block the direct route between Singapore and the invasion beaches off Siam. Deployed behind them to the north was a screen of ten submarines, which had taken station there a week before hostilities began. Two more Japanese submarines were stationed off Singapore. These could all provide sighting reports if they spotted Force Z, and could also carry out attacks on it. That, of course, would only be if the British force didn't fall foul of any of the 1,000 mines sown in the Japanese minefield on the night of 6–7 December.

The whole point of this naval operation was to screen the landing of the Japanese Army on the coast of Siam. The Japanese invasion of Malaya was to be undertaken by elements of the 25th Army, under the command of Lieutenant General Yamashito Tomoyuki. The initial landings would be carried out by elements of the 5th and 18th Infantry Divisions, and would be reinforced by the rest of their divisions, as well as by the Imperial Guard Division. This meant that the Japanese would be outnumbered during the campaign for Malaya. However, thanks to a devastating series of air attacks during the opening day of the operation, the Japanese would enjoy overwhelming air superiority in the theatre. This, and the unorthodox tactics practised by Tomoyuki's troops, together with their high morale, would more than compensate for lack of numbers. As in all areas of this campaign, the British had seriously underestimated Japanese capabilities on land, sea and air, and would pay the price.

Japanese Naval Forces, Malaya Theatre, 8–10 December 1941

Distant Cover Force (Vice-Admiral Kondo) Deployed in the South China Sea

3rd Battleship Division (elements): Battleships *Kongo* (flagship), *Haruna*
4th Cruiser Division (elements): Heavy Cruisers *Takao, Atago*
6th Destroyer Division (elements): Destroyers *Akatsuki, Hibiki*
8th Destroyer Division: Destroyers *Arashio, Asashio, Oshio, Michishio*
4th Destroyer Division: Destroyers *Maikaze, Nowake, Hagikaze*

Covering Force (Vice-Admiral Osawa) Deployed in the Gulf of Siam

Heavy Cruiser *Chokai* (flagship)
7th Cruiser Division: Heavy Cruisers *Kumano, Mikuma, Mogami, Suzuya*
11th Destroyer Division: Light Cruiser *Kashii*
Destroyers *Fubuki, Hatsuyuki, Shirayuki, Sagiri*

Amphibious Forces Deployed in the Gulf of Siam

Singora Attack Force:

Seaplane Carriers *Kamikawa Maru, Sagara Maru*
Destroyers *Amagiri, Asagiri, Yugiri, Isonamii*
13 Transport Ships, 3 Minesweepers (transporting 41st Rgt and HQ, 5th Div.)

Patani Attack Force:

2 Transport Ships, 3 Cargo Ships (transporting 42nd Rgt, 5th Div.)

Kota Bharu Attack Force:

Light Cruiser *Sendai*
12th Destroyer Division: Destroyers *Murakamo, Shinonome, Shirakumo*
19th Destroyer Division: Destroyers *Ayaname, Shikiname, Uraname*
3 Transport Ships, 1 Minesweeper (transporting 56th Rgt, 18th Div.)

DEFENDER'S CAPABILITIES

The Royal Navy's mission to Singapore

Force Z

The force the British Admiralty finally sent to the Far East was originally known as Force G. At its heart was the *Prince of Wales*, the second King George V-class battleship to enter service. She would serve as the force commander's flagship. Accompanying her was the venerable but elegant battlecruiser *Repulse*. Together, these two capital ships constituted a powerful naval force, at least in terms of surface combat. However, primarily they were being sent to Singapore as a deterrent, to discourage the Japanese from threatening British and Commonwealth interests in the region. They arrived too late to achieve this, and so were thrust into a naval campaign for which they were singularly ill-suited. Despite their impressive firepower, Force Z would have to be handled with great care to achieve anything in the face of a numerically superior enemy, and within range of enemy land-based aircraft.

The arrival of *Prince of Wales* and *Repulse* in Singapore was widely reported by both press and radio. So too had been the flagship's visits to Sierra Leone, South Africa and Ceylon, therefore the Japanese were well aware of the threat they posed, and altered their plans accordingly.

The King George V class were the first battleships to be built in Britain since the early 1920s. Designed to replace an ageing battle fleet, and laid down during the late 1930s, these ships were useful and timely additions to the fleet. However, their design had been limited by the constraints of the naval disarmament treaties of the inter-war period, and as a result their size and armament was more limited than the British Admiralty might have wished. Nevertheless, they were formidable capital ships. Their main armament consisted of ten modern 14in Mark VII guns, in three turrets, designed to fire two rounds a minute, and which had a range of 18 nautical miles. The very modernity of these guns and their mounts proved problematic, as they were prone to malfunctions. This had plagued both the *Prince of Wales* and the *King George V* during the pursuit of the German battleship *Bismarck* in May 1941. By the end of the year, though, most of these teething problems had been overcome.

As battlecruisers, the two warships of the Renown class were designed on the premise that speed and firepower were emphasised at the expense of protection. Therefore, when built, *Renown* and *Repulse* were less well protected than contemporary dreadnoughts, but

The launch of the battleship *Prince of Wales* on Merseyside in May 1939. She and her sister ship *King George V* were the first battleships to join the Royal Navy in over a decade, and were seen as thoroughly modern capital ships, despite the constraints imposed on their design by the naval disarmament treaties of the inter-war years.

at least they carried six powerful 15in guns, mounted in three twin turrets, which had a range of 14 miles. The two ships were both laid down before the battle of Jutland (1916) exposed the shortcomings of the battlecruiser – the Royal Navy lost three of them during the battle. As a result, although *Repulse* entered service in 1916, she was quickly retro-fitted with additional protection and further extensive rebuilding was carried out during the late 1930s. While she was an elderly warship, *Repulse* remained a useful capital ship, although with just six 15in guns and relatively thin armour she wasn't considered powerful to take on modern battleships such as the *Bismarck*.

Another notable difference between these two capital ships was their array of anti-aircraft defences. *Prince of Wales* carried 16 5.25in Mark I quick-firing (QF) guns, in eight twin turrets, four mounted on each side of her superstructure. As dual-purpose guns these could engage both surface and air targets, and so could elevate up to 70 deg to engage high-flying bombers. With a practical rate of fire of eight rounds a minute, a range of 22,000m (24,000 yards), and an anti-aircraft ceiling of 15,000m (49,000ft), these guns were regarded as the latest word in anti-aircraft defence. By contrast, *Repulse* was poorly served in anti-aircraft guns. She carried six obsolete 4in Mark V QF anti-aircraft guns in single mounts, bolstered by three more modern 4in Mark XV dual-purpose QF guns in triple mounts. These last pieces were dual-purpose guns, and in

This wartime diagram shows the arcs of fire of a King George V-class battleship. It says nothing of the use of the High Angle Control System (HACS) or radar to direct the fire of her anti-aircraft guns, but it clearly shows the arks of fire of her secondary guns and 'pom-poms'.

The battlecruiser *Repulse*, pictured from the decks of a troopship during her voyage from Durban to Aden in October 1941. At the time, she sported a dramatic camouflage scheme of black and light grey – a camouflage she retained until her loss in December.

anti-aircraft mode they had a range of 14,600m (16,000 yards), and a ceiling of 8,750m (28,750ft).

All these 4in and 5.25in guns were there to provide long-range anti-aircraft fire. For shorter-range protection, the Royal Navy favoured the 'Chicago piano'. This was the nickname for the eight-barrelled 2-pounder Mark VIII QF gun, or 'pom-pom'. In theory these were fully automatic, and had a range of 1,550m (1,700 yards) and could fire 100 rounds a minute, using link-fed ammunition. The trouble was that they were prone to jamming due to their complex mechanisms, and so their performance was more impressive in theory than in practice. *Prince of Wales* mounted six of these, one each on 'B' and 'Y' turrets, one on each beam abreast the forward funnel and one on each beam abreast the after one. She also mounted a four-barrelled 2-pounder Mark VII 'pom-pom'.

Repulse carried just two of these eight-barrelled 'pom-poms', one on each side of her forward funnel. Finally, *Prince of Wales* was fitted with a single 40mm Bofors gun mounted aft. This was a useful weapon, with a high rate of fire, as long as the loader could keep feeding clips of ammunition into the auto-loader. Finally, when the *Prince of Wales* stopped in Simonstown on route to Singapore, she was given seven single 20mm Oerlikons, three mounted on her quarterdeck and two on each side of the bridge. *Repulse* was given eight of them, divided equally between the same two locations. While all this array of anti-aircraft weaponry seemed

The departure of Force Z from Singapore

At 1710hrs on 8 December, Admiral Phillips' flagship *Prince of Wales* left the Singapore Naval Base, and headed out into the Jahore Strait. The battlecruiser *Repulse* followed her. Their departure was watched by hundreds of people who lined the shore to watch Force Z put to sea. After rounding Changi Point, Force Z entered the Singapore Strait, and headed east. Sunset that evening was at 1814hrs. By then the island of Singapore had fallen away astern of them, and Force Z was steering 080 deg – a little north of due east, and making 18 knots. The flagship flew an admiral's flag from her foremast, and *Repulse* followed five cables (914 metres, 1,000 yards) astern of her. Of the four escorting destroyers which made up the rest of Force Z, *Vampire* led the way, five cables ahead of the flagship, sweeping for mines as she went. The destroyer *Tenedos* followed five cables astern of the battlecruiser. Finally, the destroyers *Express* and *Electra* formed up on the port and starboard beams of the flagship, keeping four cables (732 meters, 800 yards) from her. Off to port lay the coast of Malaya – largely jungle-clad, interspersed by small villages. To starboard was the island of Bintan, while ahead lay the open sea, and a waiting enemy.

A pair of eight-barrelled 2-pounder 'pom-pom' Mark VIII mounts. These guns, sometimes nicknamed 'Chicago pianos', first entered service in 1930, but by 1941 they were considered obsolete due to their low muzzle velocity. They were also prone to jamming, and lacked the tracer or high-explosive ammunition which might have improved the value of the weapon.

fairly impressive, its effectiveness was linked closely to another all-important feature – the anti-aircraft fire control capability of these two ships.

Both *Prince of Wales* and *Repulse* were fitted with a High Angle Control System (HACS). First designed in the early 1930s, this was primarily designed to control anti-aircraft fire against high-flying bombers. It predicted where the bombers would be at a certain moment, and directed the ship's fire to intersect the bomber when it reached that spot. It was reckoned that a trained gun crew could shoot down a bomber effectively if enough rounds were fired at it.

While this was well suited to this kind of attack, it wasn't able to provide anti-aircraft direction against either dive bombers or torpedo bombers. As a result, during the late 1930s attempts were made to modify the HACS to cope with these forms of air attack. Here, a rolling barrage would be fired, forcing the enemy to either fly into it or turn away. However, in practice these modifications never lived up to the Admiralty's expectations.

The 2-pounder 'pom-pom' was fed by a steel-link belt of rounds, which in theory gave the weapon an impressive rate of fire. However, the semi-automatic hand-cranked mechanism was prone to mechanical problems, and the mounting frequently broke down while in action.

As a result, the HACS was useful against high-flying Japanese bombers, but of little value against torpedo planes which were flown with determination. It didn't help that training with British torpedo planes had led to an expectation that attacks would be conducted at slower speeds than would be the case when facing more modern aircraft. This made it difficult to place an effective barrage in the path of the approaching torpedo bombers. By late 1941, the one bright spot for the Royal Navy was the development of radar, and its integration with a ship's anti-aircraft defences. *Prince of Wales* carried a Type 279 air warning radar with a detection range of up to 95 miles. Then, when the enemy came within heavy anti-aircraft gun range, the battleship's 5.25in guns were guided by a Type 285 radar on the battleship, operating in conjunction with the HACS Mark IV. The combination improved the

The Illustrious-class fleet aircraft carrier *Indomitable* was supposed to join Admiral Phillips' force as it sailed for the Far East, but she ran aground while 'working up' in the Caribbean, and instead she was sent to the United States for repairs. Her complement of Sea Hurricanes and Fulmars would have been invaluable to Phillips.

accuracy of the whole system, although on 10 December 1941 the system's performance failed to live up to British expectations.

Both capital ships were protected against torpedo attack by a combination of armour and protective spaces. In *Prince of Wales*, the armoured belt extended 2.6m (8ft 6in) below the waterline, but this tapered to 11.4cm (4.5in) at its lower edge. Behind the outer hull was a series of compartments containing water and fuel, backed by an internal vertical torpedo bulkhead 4.5cm (1.75in) thick. *Repulse* was protected by a similar scheme, with 5.1cm (2in) of underwater protection, backed by similar fuel and water spaces, and a torpedo bulkhead 7.6cm (3in) thick. However, she had also been provided with a rounded anti-torpedo bulge, which was designed to absorb the blast of the torpedo before it hit the outer hull proper, and redirect the blast upwards. In the event, the protection of both ships proved unequal to the challenge of multiple torpedo hits.

In addition to Force Z's two capital ships, it had originally been hoped that other warships would form part of the group. However, the fleet aircraft carrier *Indomitable* ran aground in the Bahamas before she could sail for the Far East, while in Singapore, Admiral Phillips was forced to sail before other assets of the Eastern Fleet had joined him. These included the heavy cruiser *Exeter* and several destroyers. Phillips decided to leave behind the three obsolete D-class light cruisers based in Singapore, together with two old destroyers.

British Far Eastern Fleet, 10 December 1941

Commander: Admiral Phillips based on flagship
Chief of Staff: Rear-Admiral Palliser based in Singapore
Force Z (Phillips) in Gulf of Siam

Prince of Wales King George V-class battleship (Captain Leach) – fleet flagship
Repulse Renown-class battlecruiser (Captain Tennant)
Tenedos S-class destroyer (Lieutenant Dyer)
Vampire (RAN) V-class destroyer (Commander Moran RAN)
Express E-class destroyer (Lieutenant-Commander Cartwright)
Electra E-class destroyer (Commander May)

Other Forces

East Indies Squadron (Trincomalee, Ceylon): Light Aircraft Carrier *Hermes*
Heavy Cruisers *Exeter, Cornwall*
Light Cruisers *Delhi, Despatch, Diomede*

Note: *Exeter* on passage from Trincomalee to Singapore; *Hermes* in refit in Durban, South Africa; *Cornwall* in refit in Trincomalee

9th Cruiser Squadron (Singapore): Light Cruisers *Danae, Dragon, Durban*
Destroyer Division, China Station (Hong Kong): Destroyers *Scout, Stronghold, Thanet*
Far East Division (Singapore): Destroyer *Jupiter*

His escort therefore consisted of the E-class destroyers *Electra* and *Express*, which had accompanied the capital ships from Britain, the old S-class destroyer *Tenedos*, and the V-class destroyer *Vampire* of the Royal Australian Navy. The older destroyers were armed with single 4in Mark V QF guns – three on *Tenedos* and four on *Vampire*, or four single 4.7in Mark IX QF guns on the others. All carried torpedo tubes, but their anti-aircraft capability was pitiful – single 2-pounder QF 'pom-poms' on the older destroyers, and a pair of quad machine guns on the E-class vessels. Their best defence was their speed and shallow draught, and the fact that they were, after all, low priority targets.

Land and air defences

While Admiral Phillips commanded all naval forces in the region, everything else fell under the control of the Commonwealth Commander-in-Chief, Far East. From his headquarters in Singapore, Air Chief Marshal Sir Robert Brooke-Popham had to coordinate the army's defence of both Singapore and the Malay Peninsula, as well as its air defences. Planning for the defence of the region had evolved during the inter-war years, but essentially it revolved around two key premises. The first was that Singapore was vital to British strategic interests in the Far East, and so the city was developed as a naval base, and the island fortified. This involved the building of coastal batteries, to deter any naval attack, as well as providing a

OPPOSITE ANTI-AIRCRAFT DEFENCES OF *PRINCE OF WALES* AND *REPULSE*

Of the two British capital ships, only *Prince of Wales* had up-to-date anti-aircraft defences. In theory her anti-aircraft armament provided her with all-round air defence, both from long-range and close-range guns. These were supported by a High Angle Control System (HACS), dedicated fire control radars and a powerful air search radar. These, though, were incapable of defending the ship against large-scale air attacks.

Anti-aircraft armament:

16x 5.25in Dual-Purpose Quick-Firing Mark I guns in eight twin turrets

48x 2-pounder 'pom-pom' Mark VIII, in six eight-barrelled mountings

1x 40mm Bofors gun in a single mounting

7x 20mm Oerlikon AA guns in seven single mountings

In addition, on 10 December 1941, at least two single Lewis LMGs were pressed into service, mounted in the forward superstructure.

Sensors

Type 279 air search radar (mounted in foremast)

Four HACS Mark IV mountings, with Type 285 fire control radar on top. Served 5.25in guns

Four Type 282 fire control radar mountings, two on either side of bridge. Served 2-pounder guns

Repulse lacked an air search radar, and instead had to rely on her Type 284 fire control radar serving her main guns and her Type 273 surface search radar, both of which had a very limited range. Instead, she had two HACS mountings, a Type II in her foremast and a Type I aft, in her mainmast. She also lacked any form of fire control radar for her 4in guns, 'pom-poms' or machine guns.

Anti-Aircraft Armament:

6x 4in Quick-Firing Mark V AA guns in single mounts

24x 2-pounder 'pom-poms' Mark VIII, in three eight-barrelled mounts

16x 0.5in machine guns, in four quadruple mounts

8x 20mm Oerlikon AA guns in single mounts

In addition, on 10 December 1941, at least two single Lewis LMGs were pressed into service, mounted in the forward superstructure.

Sensors

Two HACS mountings – a Mark II forward and a Mark I aft

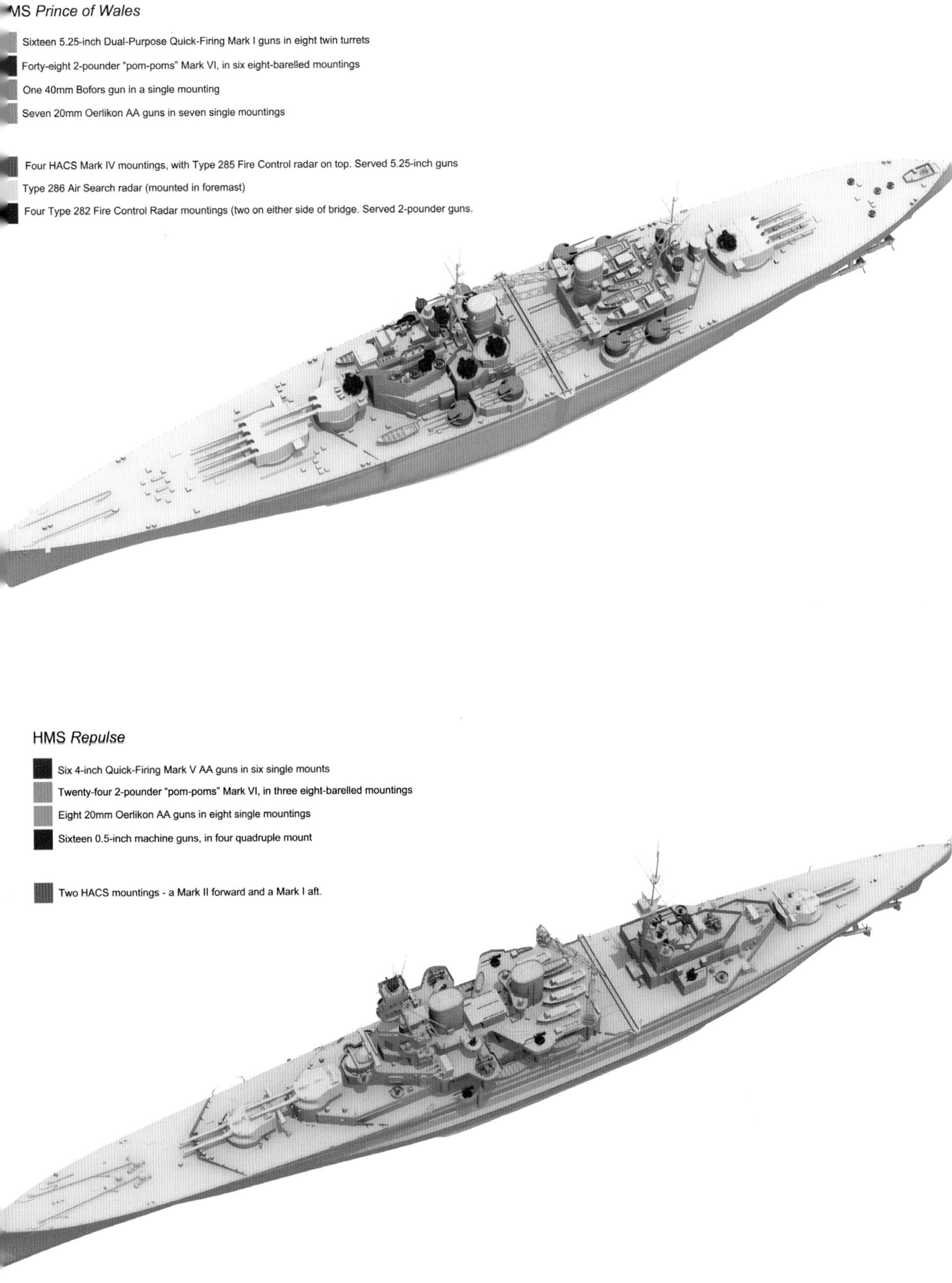
MS Prince of Wales
Sixteen 5.25-inch Dual-Purpose Quick-Firing Mark I guns in eight twin turrets
Forty-eight 2-pounder "pom-poms" Mark VI, in six eight-barelled mountings
One 40mm Bofors gun in a single mounting
Seven 20mm Oerlikon AA guns in seven single mountings
Four HACS Mark IV mountings, with Type 285 Fire Control radar on top. Served 5.25-inch guns
Type 286 Air Search radar (mounted in foremast)
Four Type 282 Fire Control Radar mountings (two on either side of bridge. Served 2-pounder guns.
HMS Repulse
Six 4-inch Quick-Firing Mark V AA guns in six single mounts
Twenty-four 2-pounder "pom-poms" Mark VI, in three eight-barelled mountings
Eight 20mm Oerlikon AA guns in eight single mountings
Sixteen 0.5-inch machine guns, in four quadruple mount
Two HACS mountings - a Mark II forward and a Mark I aft.

A squadron of Brewster Buffalo Mark I fighters in the air over the Malay Peninsula in late 1941. Had No. 453 Squadron, RAAF, been scrambled from Singapore when Force Z was off Kuantan, then Admiral Phillips' two capital ships might have been spared their fate.

strong military garrison, and a number of airfields, where fighters could be stationed to protect Singapore from enemy air attacks.

The second premise was that due to her expansionist policies, from the early 1930s on, Japan was considered the greatest threat to British interests in the Far East. As an ally, though, care was taken not to make the British position in the region so powerful that it would present a strategic threat to Japan. Singapore's defences were therefore deliberately starved of military and air assets. However, the naval base was completed in 1938, and sufficient coastal defences were installed to adequately protect Singapore from any attack from the sea. Incidentally, all but the 15in coastal guns could traverse sufficiently to bombard the landward approaches of Singapore Island, as well as its seaward approaches. The problem was, troops and aircraft earmarked for use in Singapore and Malaya were either retained in the United Kingdom, or else diverted to the Middle East.

Direct command on the land was devolved to Lieutenant General Arthur Percival, General Officer Commanding (GOC) Malayan Command. At his disposal was III Corps of the Indian Army, with two Indian infantry divisions (9th and 11th), as well as an Australian division (8th), an independent Indian brigade (12th), and various independent or local defence units. In all this force consisted of around 120,000 men. Its effectiveness need not concern us, as our focus is on the air campaign. However, despite the confidence of its leaders, this force was generally ill-prepared for what amounted to a 'blitzkrieg' campaign, where the Japanese maintained the initiative, and Commonwealth defensive capability fell apart with alarming speed.

Lieutenant-General Arthur Percival (1887–1966) had the unenviable task of commanding the British Commonwealth's ground forces in Malaya. He lacked the troops and resources he needed to adequately defend the Malay Peninsula, and protect Singapore.

The air defences of the region were under the direct control of Brooke-Popham, supported by a small group of regional commanders. In all he had 178 aircraft at his disposal, but many of these were outdated and flown by inexperienced crews. Four fighter squadrons were available, one supplied by the RAF (No. 243 Sqn), two by the RAAF (Nos. 21 and 453 Sqns) and one by the RNZAF (No. 488 Sqn). They all flew the American-designed Brewster Buffalo B-339E, which was in turn a slightly underpowered export version of the US Navy's F2A-2. The Commonwealth air forces called it the Brewster Buffalo Mark I. As a fighter, this aircraft was poorly equipped to take on its more powerful Japanese counterparts, while a lack of range limited its use in protecting naval forces for any lengthy period unless within easy reach of the fighters' home airfields. Of these, only No. 453 Squadron would be made available to provide fighter protection for Force Z when it sortied into the Gulf of Siam.

In terms of bombers, there were four squadrons of Bristol Blenheim light bombers (both Mark I and Mark IV versions), grouped into four squadrons

The Bristol Blenheim light bomber was introduced in 1937, and proved to be an effective and versatile aircraft. It was hoped to use the four squadrons in Malaya to counter any attempt at amphibious invasion, however, when it came, these squadrons were disrupted by Japanese air attacks, and no organised response to the landings was undertaken.

– Nos. 27, 34, 60 and 62 Squadrons RAF. These were effectively light bombers, with the range to pose a threat to any approaching amphibious force. However, by 1941 they were considered too vulnerable to enemy fighters, and so in most theatres they were being withdrawn from front-line service. In Malaya, though, they would be used in support of ground troops during the fighting in the Peninsula. Also available were a number of venerable Vickers Vildebeeste torpedo bombers belonging to Nos. 36 and 100 Squadrons RAF, as well as a handful of Fairey Albacore torpedo bombers attached to No. 36 Squadron.

Both of these aircraft types were biplanes, with a very limited range. The Vildebeestes were obsolete, and of little use in a modern war, but the Albacores, despite their flaws, were arguably the best torpedo plane available to the Commonwealth air forces at this stage of the war. Also available were two RAAF squadrons of Lockheed Hudson bombers, capable of being used as bomber-reconnaissance aircraft. Also available was an RAF flight of two Catalina I flying boats (designated the Consolidated PBY Catalina by its US builders), operated by No. 205 Squadron RAF. A flight of three more operated by the Dutch was also temporarily based in Singapore. With a range of more than 2,000 nautical miles, these were a useful asset to any naval commander. It made sense therefore that any naval sortie in the region would involve the support of reconnaissance flights by these flying boats.

However, their effective use required a degree of cooperation between the Royal Air Force and the Royal Navy in Malaya which simply did not exist. No coordinated tri-service defence plan was ever instituted before the outbreak of hostilities. Instead, cooperation was given on an ad hoc basis, with Admiral Phillip's deputy, Rear-Admiral Palliser, serving as the link between Force Z, Brooke-Popham and the RAF. The Japanese invasion threw any nascent plans into disarray. First, the bombing and strafing of RAF airfields in the Malayan Peninsula proved highly successful, destroying or damaging most of these Commonwealth air assets in the first 24 hours of the invasion. What remained was thrown into the fighting to protect the hard-pressed land units in northern Malaya. As a result, apart from reconnaissance flights by Catalinas, and the dedicated support of the Buffalos of No. 453 Squadron, the Royal Navy were left to their own devices.

Rear-Admiral Arthur Palliser (left) and Admiral Sir Tom Phillips, waiting on the quayside in Singapore for the arrival of *Prince of Wales* and *Repulse*. At that stage, just days before the outbreak of hostilities, Phillips still believed these capital ships would deter the Japanese from launching any attack on Singapore or Malaya.

CAMPAIGN OBJECTIVES

The imperial rivals

The Japanese

The Brewster Buffalo Mark I fighter performed poorly when compared to the latest Japanese 'Zero' fighters, but were certainly adequate to the task of providing air cover to Force Z against bombers. These aircraft, deployed at RAF Sembawang at Singapore, are from No. 21 Squadron, RAAF.

Japan did well out of World War I, gaining former German colonies in China and the Pacific, and establishing a small foothold in Manchuria. From 1930 on, Japanese foreign policy was increasingly dominated by military factions. In 1931 this influence led to the Japanese invasion of Manchuria, and the Japanese army became embroiled in a full-scale war on the Chinese mainland. A military coup in 1932 effectively handed control of the Japanese government to the military, and disregarding world opinion, the Japanese embarked on an even more ambitious policy of territorial expansion. This was supported by a huge increase in military expenditure, and in the creation of a powerful, modern fleet. In 1937, after a brief ceasefire, the Sino-Japanese War erupted again, and Japanese troops captured both Peking (Beijing) and Nanking.

The Western powers were appalled by reports of Japanese atrocities, but they did little to stop the war. This was regarded as a sign of weakness by the Japanese, and encouraged planners to consider the creation of a Greater East Asia Co-Prosperity Sphere. The premise was simple. Japan lacked the raw materials it needed to fuel its industrial and military expansion, and had to import raw materials such as oil and iron. This Co-Prosperity Sphere was expected to solve this by seizing control of territory rich in these raw materials, and so, from 1939 on, plans were drawn up for a hugely ambitious military operation on several fronts, from Burma to the Gilbert Islands. This territory included areas such as Malaya and the Philippines, which were under British or American control. These plans would, potentially, set Japan and these two Western powers on a course to war.

In July 1939, as a result of Japan's undermining of American interests in China, the United States pulled out of an American–Japanese trade treaty. The following year the US government issued an act which severely limited the export of 'essential defense materials' to Japan. This included oil, steel and iron ore – the imported goods Japan desperately needed in order to maintain its military programme. The Japanese response was to continue diplomatic

On 9 December the Japanese Kaidai-class submarine I-65 was one of ten boats strung out in a series of patrol lines spanning the southern approaches to the Gulf of Siam. Her sighting of Force Z alerted the Japanese to the threat the British force posed to their invasion plans.

negotiations, in an attempt to lift these restrictions, and to increase trade. Meanwhile, the Japanese military stepped up their plans for what was increasingly seen as a vital military solution to this geopolitical impasse. What emboldened them was the realisation that with Britain embroiled in a war with both Nazi Germany and their Italian allies, the country's possessions in the Far East would have to fend for themselves.

By late 1941, while negotiations to lift the economic embargo continued, the final arrangements were being made to this great venture. It was decided that if no agreement with the United States was reached by 29 November, then this plan would be set in motion. The deadline passed and so, on 1 December, General Tojo confirmed that this meant Japan would go to war on 8 December 1941. By then the Japanese military machine was fully prepared for this eventuality, and all necessary deployments had been made. In effect, the plan involved the launching of five simultaneous operations:

1. An attack on the US Pacific Fleet based at Pearl Harbor in Hawaii. Due to the International Date Line, this attack would take place at dawn on Sunday 7 December. A Japanese force of six aircraft carriers and 360 aircraft were already en route to Hawaii.
2. At the same time, on Sunday 8 December, a large-scale invasion of the American-owned Philippines would be launched, supported by massed air attacks from Japanese airfields in Formosa. These air attacks would concentrate on destroying American aircraft, thereby ensuring air superiority over the archipelago.
3. In the Central Pacific, Japanese invasion forces, supported by powerful naval forces would attack and seize the American-owned islands of Guam and Wake, as well as the Gilbert Islands. Then, airfields would be established there to cut off American lines of communication between Hawaii and the Philippines.
4. Japanese forces would seize the British enclave of Hong Kong.
5. At the same time, Japanese troops would be landed on the coast of Siam. The troops would then advance southwards into Malaya, and advance down the Malay Peninsula to Singapore, which would be taken by land assault. This operation would be supported by naval forces, and by aircraft operated by both the army and the navy.

The Japanese Takao-class heavy cruiser *Chokai*, flagship of Vice-Admiral Ozawa's Covering Force, was conventionally armed with eight 8in guns, but like the other destroyers and cruisers in this force, she also carried Type 93 'Long Lance' torpedoes, carried in the launcher shown here.

The heavy cruiser *Exeter*, which fought off the *Graf Spee* at the battle of the River Plate (1939) was part of the British Eastern Fleet, but Force Z sailed from Singapore while the cruiser was still en route there from Ceylon. If she had been there, she might well have been a third casualty.

This, however, was only the first phase of the operation. If successful, the Japanese would continue their drive into the Dutch East Indies, Borneo and New Guinea. This was as much about seizing oil fields as it was about creating a defensible perimeter to Japan's new sphere of influence. After the capture of Singapore the Japanese army would also drive west from Siam into Burma, which would bring it to the very borders of British India. It was expected that these operations could take six months to complete. In the process they would have dismantled British, American and Dutch colonial spheres of interest in South-East Asia and the East Indies. The hope then was that this spectacular success would be followed by a period of consolidation, backed up by renewed diplomatic negotiation, in order to secure a lasting peace. This time, though, the Japanese would be the ones negotiating from a position of strength.

The invasion of Malaya

The Japanese plan was simple, bold and calculated. Earlier that year, the Japanese had gained possession of French Indochina. Now the country would be used as a springboard for the invasion. Army Air Force squadrons would concentrate their efforts on destroying Commonwealth aircraft on the ground, and on rendering their airfields inoperable. Naval land-based air units would protect the transport groups, cover the landings and also stand by to counter any British naval counter-attack in the Gulf of Siam. To this end the 22nd Air Flotilla, operating from airfields around Saigon, was well placed to carry out all these missions. The transport force would sail from Cam Ranh Bay, to the north of Saigon, screened by Vice-Admiral Kondo's naval forces. The landing was timed to coincide with the other attacks in the great Japanese plan, which meant hostilities would begin on 7 December.

The army would land its first wave of troops inside the Kingdom of Siam, close to the northern border of British-held Malaya. Another force would attack Kota Bharu, on the Malay border. The Japanese troops would then move quickly to seal off the Malay Peninsula from the north. As overland lines of communication were established with French Indochina, the bulk of the landing force would swing south, to engage the Commonwealth forces defending the Malay border. The Corps-sized Japanese force charged with this operation was composed of veteran troops, blooded in the fighting in China. They were all versed in jungle warfare, and it was expected that they would quickly prevail over their less experienced Indian Army and Australian opponents. The Japanese would then continue their drive on Singapore.

The naval operations began on the night of 6–7 December, as over 1,000 mines were laid between Tioman and the Anamba Islands, to block the direct route from Singapore into the

Gulf of Siam. Submarines were also deployed as a patrol screen, to advise of any British naval sortie. Then, powerful naval units under Kondo and his deputy Vice-Admiral Ozawa would screen the landing sites. Once the troops were landed, the transports would return to Cam Ranh Bay, where a second wave of troops would embark. Above all, the Japanese would also be able to draw on their powerful force of naval land-based bombers, to attack any British naval counter-attack, and to support the invasion force. The Japanese priority, though, was to ensure that the amphibious operation was a success.

At 0045hrs on 8 December, the first landings began at Kota Bharu. Across the Pacific, and on the other side of the International Date Line, the first bombs fell on Pearl Harbor at 0753hrs on 7 December. Therefore, taking into account time zones and the date line, the invasion of Malaya preceded Pearl Harbor by an hour. Despite British search aircraft having spotted the transport fleet the day before, poor communication meant that nothing had been done to intercept it before the landings began. While Commonwealth aircraft scrambled to attack the ships at dawn, and even managed to sink one of them, their efforts were largely thwarted by Japanese air superiority. Dawn strikes on Commonwealth airfields in northern Malaya by the 22nd Air Flotilla took the defenders by surprise. At 0400hrs that morning, a small raid was even carried out on Singapore. Prepared or not, the British Commonwealth and Imperial Japan were now at war.

The British

During World War I, Britain and Japan had been allies, and the two countries enjoyed cordial relations. However, during the late 1920s cracks began appearing in this unity, as the British came to regard the Japanese as a potential military threat to their interests in the Far East. The naval cuts of the post-war years and the economic slump that followed, limited the ability of Britain to maintain extensive military and naval forces in the region. Therefore, while Britain relied heavily on India, Australia and New Zealand for military support, it also scaled down its own naval presence on the China Station. Unrest in China led to the realisation that Hong Kong was no longer a secure base in the region, so the British government looked to Singapore as its new bastion in the region. A new naval base was established there, and Singapore Island was fortified, rendering it virtually safe from seaborne attack. Churchill went so far as to describe it as 'The Gibraltar of the East'. The naval base there was finally opened in 1938.

The E-class destroyer *Express* formed part of the *Prince of Wales'* escort from Britain, and also accompanied her during her sortie into the Gulf of Siam. She was also on hand at the end, to rescue survivors from the sinking flagship.

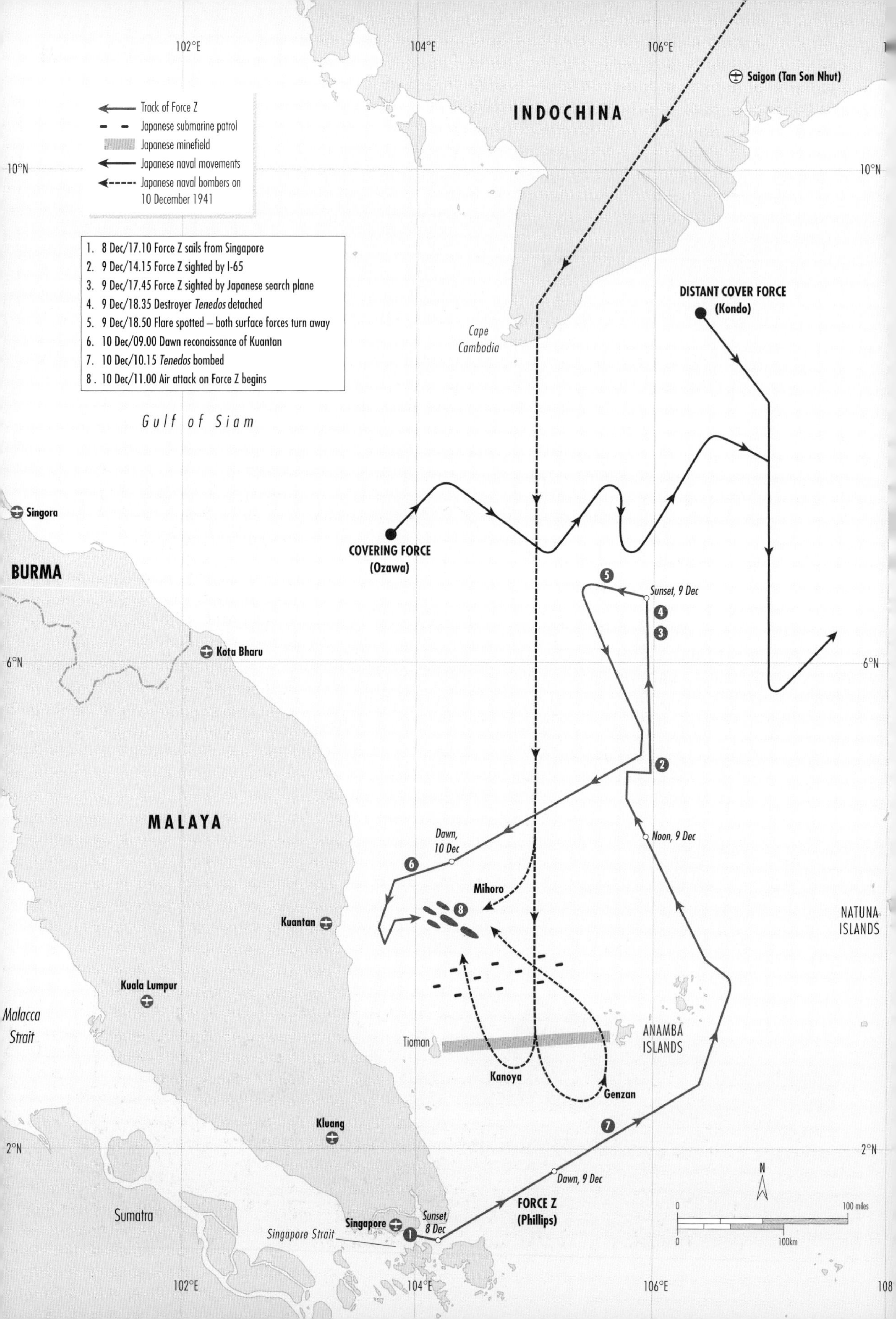

102°E
104°E
106°E
10°N
6°N
2°N
108
Track of Force Z
Japanese submarine patrol
Japanese minefield
Japanese naval movements
Japanese naval bombers on 10 December 1941
1. 8 Dec/17.10 Force Z sails from Singapore
2. 9 Dec/14.15 Force Z sighted by I-65
3. 9 Dec/17.45 Force Z sighted by Japanese search plane
4. 9 Dec/18.35 Destroyer *Tenedos* detached
5. 9 Dec/18.50 Flare spotted – both surface forces turn away
6. 10 Dec/09.00 Dawn reconaissance of Kuantan
7. 10 Dec/10.15 *Tenedos* bombed
8 . 10 Dec/11.00 Air attack on Force Z begins
INDOCHINA
Saigon (Tan Son Nhut)
DISTANT COVER FORCE (Kondo)
Cape Cambodia
Gulf of Siam
Singora
BURMA
COVERING FORCE (Ozawa)
Sunset, 9 Dec
Kota Bharu
MALAYA
Noon, 9 Dec
Dawn, 10 Dec
Mihoro
Kuantan
NATUNA ISLANDS
Kuala Lumpur
Malacca Strait
Tioman
ANAMBA ISLANDS
Kanoya
Genzan
Kluang
Dawn, 9 Dec
N
0
100 miles
100km
Sumatra
Singapore
Sunset, 8 Dec
FORCE Z (Phillips)
Singapore Strait

OPPOSITE OPERATIONS IN THE GULF OF SIAM, 8–10 DECEMBER 1941

The problem, though, was that, apart from the cruisers and destroyers usually deployed on the China Station, there was no matching naval presence at Singapore. Instead, the Admiralty intended to send a naval force from Britain to reinforce Singapore in time of war. In 1922 it was estimated that, if attacked, Singapore would have to hold out for 42 days before these warships arrived, but, following the outbreak of the war in Europe in 1939, this period was increased to six months. There were other problems too. The Singapore garrison lacked the troops it needed to properly defend itself, so the British Chiefs of Staff decided that, to buy time in case of attack, the entire Malay Peninsula had to be defended. This was doubly necessary as there were several airfields in the Malay Peninsula, including those on its northern border at Kota Bharu, Gong Kedah and Machang, which were well-placed to dominate the seaward approaches to the Peninsula.

By the late 1930s, it was clear that Japanese military expansion represented the biggest threat to British interests in the region. However, little attempt was made to reinforce the troops and squadrons needed to defend Malaya, or to establish a powerful and permanent naval presence at Singapore. Instead, it was felt that any such reinforcement would be seen by the Japanese as an aggressive move, and so increase hostility. Still, some progress was made. In February 1941, an Australian division arrived in Malaya, to reinforce the Corps of Indian Army troops stationed in the country. A few extra squadrons of aircraft also arrived, but the war in Europe and the Middle East was considered a greater priority, so what aircraft did appear were virtually obsolete.

By mid-1940 the situation had become so serious that the Chiefs of Staff compiled a report which concluded that sufficient reinforcements of troops, aircraft and warships were unlikely

The light aircraft carrier *Hermes* was part of Britain's Eastern Fleet in December 1941. Although she could only carry 20 aircraft, she would have been a useful addition to Force Z. However, in early December she was deployed in the South Atlantic, hunting fruitlessly for German raiders.

As the Admiralty's First Sea Lord, Admiral of the Fleet Sir Dudley Pound (1877–1943) was opposed to sending *Prince of Wales* and *Repulse* to the Far East. He considered the force too weak to serve as much of a deterrent. However, he finally gave in to Churchill's demands, and reluctantly agreed to the deployment.

to reach Singapore until the military situation in the Middle East improved. However, the ship carrying this report to Singapore was intercepted by a German commerce raider, and the Germans duly passed it to the Japanese. This frank precis of Commonwealth weakness in Malaya only served to embolden the Japanese, who by then were already planning to attack the Peninsula. Thanks to it, they realised the operation would be less risky than they had imagined. The military situation deteriorated further in mid-1941 when the Japanese gained control of French Indochina. Now, Japanese aircraft were within striking range of Singapore, and so Commonwealth air superiority over Malaya could no longer be guaranteed.

This led to more calls to reinforce Malaya. Both Prime Minister Churchill and the Chiefs of Staff applied pressure on the Admiralty to do something to reinforce Britain's position in the Far East. In May 1941 the threat posed by the *Bismarck* was overcome – a naval campaign that 'blooded' the *Prince of Wales* – but that simply increased Churchill's enthusiasm to send two capital ships to Singapore. Finally, on 20 October, the Admiralty ceded to his demands and agreed to send two capital ships – the new battleship *Prince of Wales*, and the elderly battlecruiser *Repulse*. However, the Admiralty insisted that the force needed air cover, and added the fleet aircraft carrier *Indomitable* to the force. *Prince of Wales* left Scapa Flow a few days later, and put in to Greenock on the Clyde, to pick up the force's new commander, Admiral Tom Phillips. Then, accompanied by the destroyers *Electra*, *Express*, *Hesperus* and *Legion*, Phillips led what was now known as Force G on the first leg of its voyage to the Far East.

Admiral Sir Tom Phillips (1888–1941) was an experienced naval officer, who served on destroyers during World War I, and assumed his first command in 1928. However, for much of the inter-war period, Phillips served as a staff officer, 'commanding a desk' in the Admiralty. He reached flag rank in January 1939, while serving as a naval adviser to King George VI.

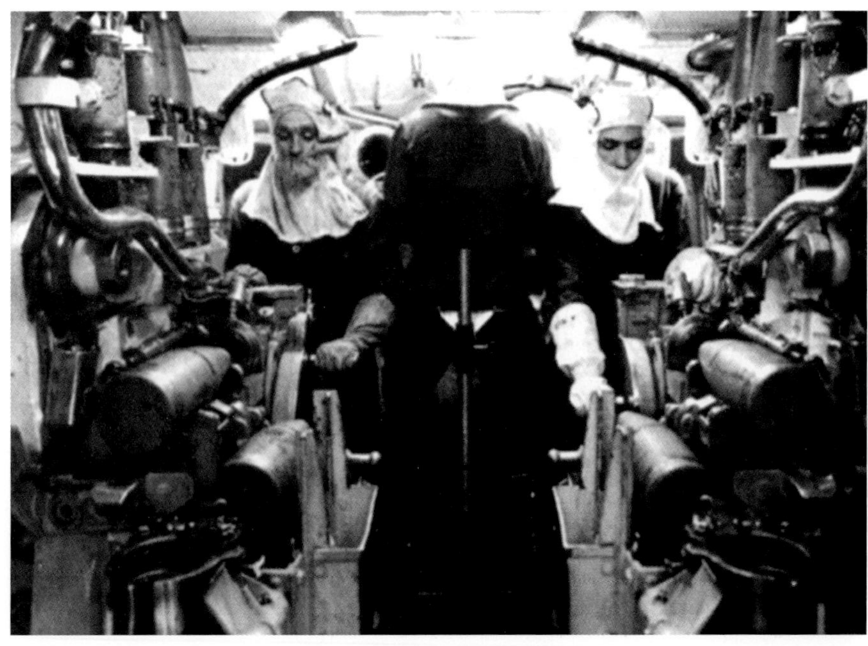

The cramped interior of one of the eight twin 5.25in dual-purpose QF Mark I gun turrets mounted in *Prince of Wales*. The calibre was chosen as it was the largest calibre that could be physically loaded by its crew. Unfortunately, the guns had a lower rate of fire than anticipated, while the turret training and elevating speeds were unsuited to the tracking of fast, modern aircraft.

HMS *Prince of Wales*, pictured in the afternoon of 2 December 1941, as she arrived in Singapore Naval Base. Her battered hull paintwork betrays the rigours of her long voyage from Britain. In the background is the light cruiser *Mauritius*, then undergoing major engine repairs.

As Vice Chief of the Naval Staff he got on well with Churchill, and further promotion followed, until he became a full Admiral in October 1941 and was named as the new Commander-in-Chief of the Eastern Fleet. By taking Force G to sea he was effectively returning to active seagoing duties himself. A small man – his men nicknamed him 'Tom Thumb' – Phillips was also a keen advocate of old-style sea power. He was reportedly unimpressed by the threat posed to his ships by Japanese aircraft. Soon enough, he would witness the effectiveness of naval air strikes at first hand.

On 5 November, Force G put in to Freetown in Sierra Leone. By now *Hesperus* and *Legion*, which were needed in home waters had been replaced by the destroyer *Jupiter*, which was also bound for the Far East. While in West Africa, Phillips learned that *Indomitable* had been damaged, and so was unable to join his force. Still, he pressed on, and on 15 November the *Prince of Wales* steamed into Cape Town, in South Africa. After two days the force continued on into the Indian Ocean, and on 28 November it reached Colombo in Ceylon (now Sri Lanka), after refuelling en route. The *Repulse* was already in the Indian Ocean, and on 29 November she put out from Trincomalee, to rendezvous with Force G to the south-east of Ceylon. The naval group was now complete.

Phillips, though, wasn't there to see it – he flew on ahead to Singapore to meet key Commonwealth officers, including Air Chief Marshal Brooke-Popham. Finally, on 2 December, *Prince of Wales*, *Repulse* and their attendant destroyers arrived in Singapore. Churchill had had his way, and Singapore had finally become a naval base worthy of the name. These reinforcements certainly arrived at an opportune moment. During the voyage out international tensions had increased dramatically. Now, a war with Japan was seen as all but inevitable. Admiral Phillips would have to take command of a fleet, bring it to readiness, consult his Allies, try to discover Japanese intentions and come up with a plan for the defence of Malaya. He didn't know it yet, but he'd almost run out of time.

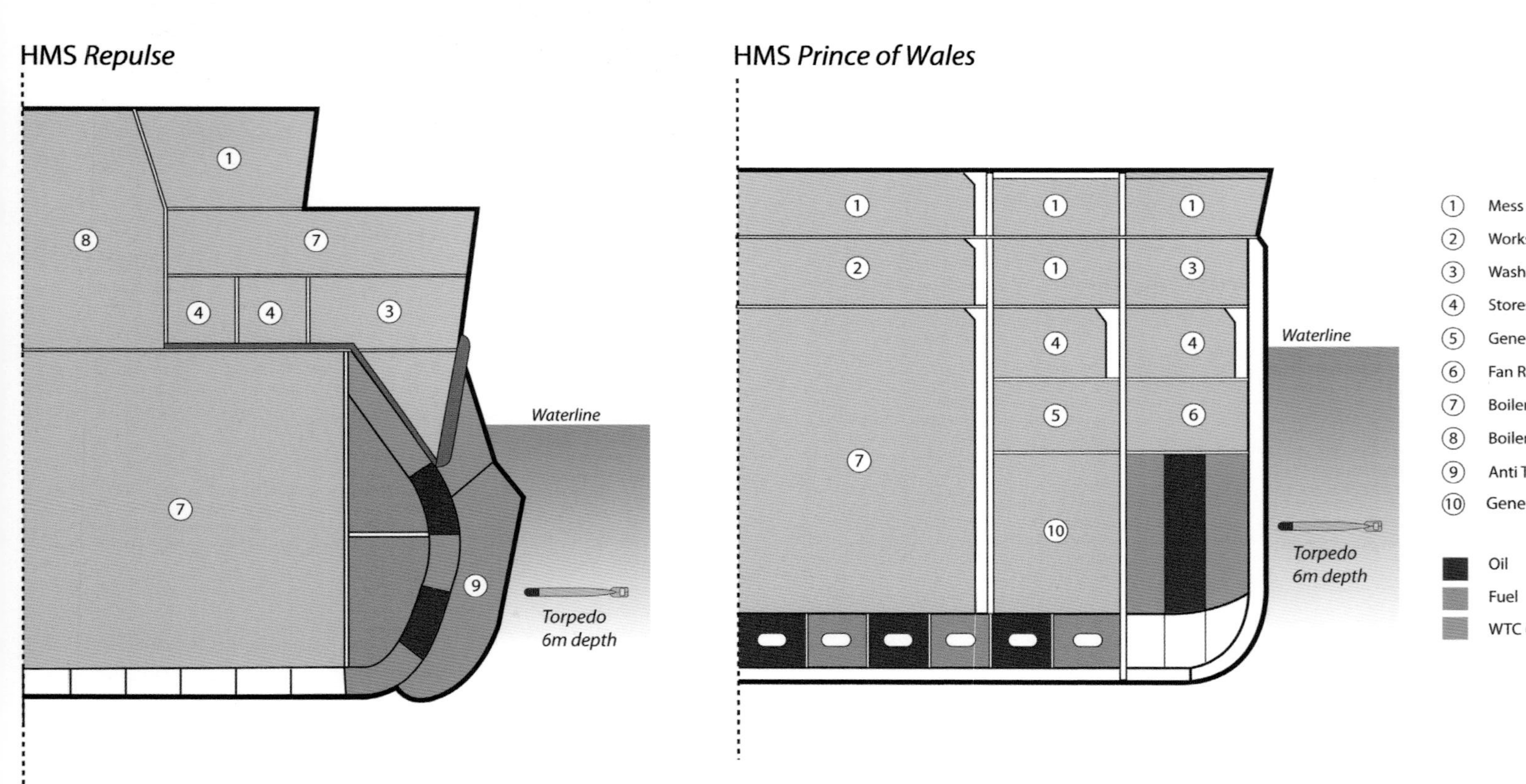
HMS *Repulse*
Waterline
Torpedo 6m depth
HMS *Prince of Wales*
Waterline
Torpedo 6m depth
1 Mess Deck
2 Workshop
3 Washrooms
4 Stores
5 Generator Room
6 Fan Room
7 Boiler Room
8 Boiler Upatakes
9 Anti Torpedo bulge
10 Generator Room
Oil
Fuel
WTC (Void Watertight Compartment)

OPPOSITE FORCE Z UNDERWATER PROTECTION AGAINST TORPEDOES

Both *Prince of Wales* and *Repulse* had different forms of underwater protection against mines and torpedoes.
Repulse, built during World War I but modernised in the mid-1930s, relied on an anti-torpedo bulge to prematurely detonate a torpedo before it struck the ship's outer hull. Beyond it was another inner anti-torpedo bulge. The spaces inboard of it were either filled with fuel oil, or were empty voids – watertight compartments. Inboard of these a pair of thin vertical bulkheads formed a 'sandwich', with a thin void between them. This was designed as a last line of defence against a torpedo explosion.
Prince of Wales, which entered service in 1941, employed a different form of protection. Here, the armoured belt protecting the outside of the hull extended lower, and a torpedo would detonate against it. At its lowest portion this armour was 5.4in thick. Further inboard, the vertical 'sandwich' of bulkheads was replaced by a torpedo bulkhead 2in thick. The area between it and the outer hull was composed of three spaces, with one containing fuel oil sandwiched between two watertight compartments.

The day the warships arrived, US reconnaissance planes had sighted a concentration of 21 Japanese transport ships in Cam Ranh Bay. It also reported the arrival of more aircraft to Saigon. Then, a British patrol sighted a pack of ten Japanese submarines on the surface, off Cambodia Point, heading towards Singapore. The Admiralty suggested moving the capital ships out of enemy reach, but the *Prince of Wales* was already in dry dock, undergoing a routine hull cleaning. Instead he sent *Repulse* on a goodwill visit to Darwin in Australia, accompanied by *Vampire* and *Tenedos*. Meanwhile, Phillips asked the Admiralty for reinforcements, to increase the deterrent value of his fleet. The following day, Phillips flew to Manila in the Philippines, to meet Admiral Hart and General MacArthur, the American commanders in the archipelago. This was meant to be the start of a series of meetings, to coordinate military actions between the British, American and Dutch forces in the region.

Admiral Phillips remained in Manila until late on Saturday 6 December. He returned with the promise of four US destroyers, and agreed to move his three destroyers in Hong Kong back to Singapore. Before he left, though, word reached Phillips that the Japanese transports were at sea, and were heading south. The sighting report from an Australian Hudson bomber also reported that they were accompanied by a battleship, five cruisers and seven destroyers – the Japanese were on the move. Their destination was still unknown, but Phillips had to consider it likely they were heading towards Malaya. He immediately recalled *Repulse* from Darwin to Singapore, and ordered *Prince of Wales* to prepare to sail. He planned to sortie into the Gulf of Siam once *Repulse* joined him. Meanwhile extra air searches were requested from the RAF in Malaya, although, for now, bad weather was screening the Japanese ships.

Phillips landed back in Singapore early on Sunday 7 December. The day was spent meeting Brooke-Popham and other senior officers, to discuss the

Air Chief Marshal Sir Robert Brooke-Popham (1878–1953) was the senior British military figure in Malaya, and the man charged with the defence of both Malaya and Singapore. However, he had no direct line of communication with Admiral Phillips, who answered directly to the Admiralty in London.

A single-mounted 4in anti-aircraft gun, covering the starboard beam of *Repulse*. The eight guns fitted in the battlecruiser were outdated, and lacked the punch of more modern weaponry. At one stage the battlecruiser had carried twin mounts, but these were removed in 1938 to provide additional accommodation during a Royal cruise, and were never replaced.

OPPOSITE
The Royal Australian Navy's destroyer *Vampire* formed part of Force Z during its sortie into the Gulf of Siam. This elderly V-class destroyer first entered service during World War I, and so she lacked modern anti-aircraft weaponry. Her prime role in the force was as an anti-submarine escort.

extent of the threat facing Malaya. They were all now fairly convinced the Japanese invasion force was heading their way, although so far it hadn't been re-located. By the evening, Phillips had decided that his best course was to put to sea, to intercept the Japanese. He said as much in a signal to the Admiralty that evening, adding that his attack would be made in conjunction with land-based air attacks. At least the arrival of *Repulse* that afternoon gave him a naval force powerful enough to intervene. However, by then, unknown to anyone in Singapore, the Japanese were poised to launch their attacks, everywhere from Malaya to Pearl Harbor.

It was early on Monday 8 December that word of the landings first reached Phillips in the naval base. These landings at Kota Bharu and further up the coast began at 0045hrs, before the dawn attack on Pearl Harbor was unleashed. From that moment on, Britain and the Commonwealth was at war with Japan. The military situation deteriorated rapidly. The Japanese established their beachhead at Kota Bharu, and overran the airfield. Other airfields in northern Malaya were pounded by heavy air attacks, and further landings in Siam cut the Malay Peninsula off from the north.

Soon, similar news reached the naval base from Hong Kong, the Philippines and Hawaii. Singapore even found itself under air attack, although this achieved little. The admiral, though, was only able to intervene at sea. He was clearly too late to stop the landings, but at least his naval force could sortie and try to sink the transports as they returned to Indochina. Throughout the day his small staff busied themselves planning for this venture, and the warships were readied for sea. At 1230hrs, Admiral Phillips held a planning meeting on board the *Prince of Wales*. Nobody from Malay Command attended, or any representatives of the Commonwealth air forces. Instead, the meeting was a purely naval affair. Attending it were Phillips' Chief of Staff, Rear-Admiral Palliser, as well as Captains Leach and Tennant, from the *Prince of Wales* and the *Repulse*. Also there were the captains of the destroyers selected as their escorts.

At this meeting, Phillips outlined his options, and his plan. Most of these options were quickly dismissed – remaining in port, or sailing to a port safe from air attack. Instead, the admiral told the assembly he intended to sortie into the Gulf of Siam, where he would try to intercept the Japanese transports. He added that Palliser would remain ashore in Singapore, to liaise between the naval group – now redesignated as 'Force Z' – and the land and air forces in Malaya, as well as the Admiralty. Phillips would request air support from the RAF, as well as reconnaissance flights, to search ahead of the force for enemy submarines, and to locate the Japanese naval groups in the northern part of the gulf. However, no formal arrangements were made with the air force. This was left to Palliser to arrange with his RAF counterparts.

Phillips revealed that he expected to intercept the enemy somewhere to the west of Singora at dawn on 10 December. Reports of the newly laid minefield west of the Anamba

HMS *Tenedos* was one of four elderly destroyers stationed in Hong Kong in late 1941. She was an S-class destroyer, commissioned just after World War I, and had served in the Far East since 1938. After being detached from Force Z she was attacked by Japanese aircraft while returning alone to Singapore.

Islands had reached him, so he intended to pass to the east of this archipelago before heading north towards the Japanese. He also stressed the importance of keeping an eye out for Japanese submarines, after passing on the report that at least ten had been sighted heading into the Gulf of Siam before the outbreak of hostilities. Lieutenant Dyer of the destroyer *Tenedos* described the meeting as a calm, thoughtful one, and that Phillips likened the venture to the Home Fleet venturing into the Skaggerak, between German-occupied Norway and Denmark, without any air cover. Everyone knew it was a risky venture, but like Phillips, the mood was that something had to be done to relieve pressure on the other services.

When the planning meeting ended, the officers returned to their ships, and completed their last-minute preparations. Some, including Leach and Tennant, enjoyed a last few hours ashore. Palliser, though, was occupied drafting a request for air support, which he passed to Air Vice Marshal Pulford, who commanded the hard pressed Commonwealth air forces in Malaya. In it, he asked for reconnaissance flights ahead of the naval force during 9 December, and a thorough air reconnaissance of the beachhead at Singora the following morning. Finally, he asked for fighter protection over the naval force, in the vicinity of Singora, that same morning. Both Palliser and Pulford realised, however, that by then there might not be much of an air force left. Still, by now Phillips was committed to the venture. Force Z would put to sea that evening, shortly after 1900hrs. The die was cast.

THE CAMPAIGN

The last day of the big-gun battleship

Force Z sorties

The Mitsubishi Type 96 G3M bomber formed the backbone of Japan's land-based naval air squadrons in Indochina. These bombers had their faults, but they still possessed the range and capability to attack any enemy force entering the Gulf of Siam.

At 1710hrs on Monday 8 December, Force Z began leaving harbour. The elderly destroyers *Tenedos* and *Vampire* were the first to depart, followed by *Repulse* and *Prince of Wales*. The destroyers *Electra* and *Express* were already at sea, having spent the day honing their minesweeping skills. They would rendezvous with the rest of the force later, after it passed Changi Point. After clearing Singapore Naval Base this procession of four warships turned into the main channel of the Jahore Strait. It was a hot and humid evening, but as the ships left shortly before sunset, hundreds of spectators lined the shore to watch them leave. Earlier that day, Singapore had been subjected to its first ever air raid. The Pacific War had already come to the island and none of the onlookers would have doubted that these warships were sailing into battle. The more skilled observers would also have noticed that *Prince of Wales* was flying the flag of an admiral.

On the battleship's bridge, Admiral Phillips watched as they passed the harbour's defensive boom, and entered the Singapore Strait. There the two remaining destroyers were waiting for them, and as the force set a course towards the south-east, Singapore dwindled away astern of them. Once safely in the middle of the Singapore Strait, Phillips ordered that they take up their cruising formation. The two capital ships formed up in line astern, with the flagship *Prince of Wales* in front, and *Repulse* following four cables (800yds, or 731m) astern of her. Eight cables ahead of the flagship was the destroyer *Electra*, sweeping the channel for mines, while the remaining three destroyers formed a screen on each beam and astern of the two capital ships. Originally, *Express* had been designated as the minesweeper, but her gear malfunctioned soon after they assumed their cruising formation and so *Electra* took her place. In this manner they set off to war, making a leisurely 17.5 knots.

Overall, morale was high on board the warships. However, afterwards, some Repulses recalled a sense of foreboding, based mostly on the largely unearned reputation of the *Prince of Wales* as 'a Jonah', an unlucky ship. During the evening they passed the Horsburgh Light, marking the eastern end of the strait, and Phillips ordered the formation to set a course towards the north-east, to pass to the east of the Anamba Islands. Phillips already knew that the Japanese had been laying mines between the islands and the Malay mainland, so he planned to keep well clear of this passage, even though it offered a more direct route to his objective. Despite the fact that he was unaware of the screen of Japanese submarines deployed to the north of the minefield, he knew a group of them had been spotted heading into the Gulf of Siam. The presence of enemy submarines therefore remained a distinct possibility, and with it the risk of being sighted, or worse, attacked.

Shortly before 2300hrs, the radio room on board the *Prince of Wales* received a long incoming message. It was the latest intelligence brief for the admiral from Rear-Admiral Arthur Palliser, his Chief of Staff, who had been left behind at the Navy Base to coordinate communications between Force Z and Brooke-Popham, the Admiralty and the local Royal Air Force squadrons who were expected to provide Phillips with air cover. Palliser's report made disturbing reading. Sent at 2253hrs, it confirmed that from 0800hrs the following morning, the RAF would be flying air searches over the north-west of Force Z, extending over 100 miles ahead of them. However, only one Catalina flying boat was available to carry out the search. This was not even close to being sufficient for a thorough search, but given the disasters befalling the Commonwealth squadrons in Malaya, it was probably all that Phillips could have expected.

The message also told him that on Wednesday 10 December, when he reached his hunting area off the Japanese beachheads, he would be operating on his own, without any air cover. The military news was equally depressing – Kota Bharu airfield had been overrun, and others were under attack from Japanese bombers. The Japanese landings seemed to have been successful, and the situation at Kota Bharu, according to Palliser, 'does not seem good'. Force Z, therefore, would be very much on its own, both during its surprise attack on the Japanese, and also throughout its withdrawal back to Singapore. Palliser's message also reminded Admiral Phillips of the large number of Japanese land-based bombers stationed in Southern Indonesia. He added that Air Chief Marshal Brooke-Popham had requested that the Americans in the Philippines carry out bombing raids on these airfields. Like the British admirals, he was completely unaware that by then the Americans were facing an invasion of their own.

The *Prince of Wales*, pictured departing from the Singapore Naval Base in the early evening of 8 December 1941. The sailing of Force Z was watched by hundreds of onlookers, but there is no clear evidence it was reported to the Japanese.

Having considered this, Phillips decided to stick to his original plan. That evening, the previously clear skies had gone, and the forecast predicted low clouds and rain squalls for much of the following day. In other words, it was the perfect weather conditions for the British, as it should shield them from Japanese reconnaissance planes. By continuing on towards the north during the day, by nightfall they would be at the same latitude as the invasion beaches. Then, with a high-speed run to the west, they could fall upon the Japanese and, after inflicting the maximum possible damage to transports and escorts, they would turn south again, and speed away to safety. With luck the same low cloud would help screen them during their withdrawal too. The whole plan, therefore, depended on bad weather to screen their approach and escape, and remaining undetected throughout the following day.

In fact, despite Palliser's message, Brooke-Popham hadn't abandoned Force Z altogether. The Brewster Buffalos of No. 453 Squadron, RAAF, based at Sembawang airfield outside Singapore were tasked with supporting the British naval force. While it lacked the strength to provide a proper combat air patrol over Force Z, it was there if required. This in itself was a sacrifice, as at that moment every available fighter was needed to protect the airfields in northern Malaya. Unfortunately, no workable plan for air support had been arranged. The hope was that the air search radars fitted in the British capital ships would give adequate warning of any Japanese air attack. Then, No. 453 Squadron would be scrambled, and would speed north to do what it could to fend off the enemy bombers. This, though, was an arrangement at odds with the basic arithmetic of speeds and ranges, and the very limited effectiveness of the British radar.

Through the night, Force Z maintained its course, speed and formation. By dawn, just after 0600hrs on Tuesday 9 December, they were still on a north-easterly course, 180 nautical miles from the Horsburgh Light, and approximately 25 miles to the south-east of Pulau Bajau in the Anamba Islands. Admiral Phillips and his staff were pleased by the low cloud and mist that covered the sea, and by the occasional rain squalls. It would all help to reduce the risk of detection by the enemy. That morning they had roughly 500 miles to steam before reaching the likely location of the Japanese. All Phillips had to do was to remain undetected until nightfall, in a little over 12 hours' time. He had already known about the hastily laid

The *Repulse*, pictured shortly before the outbreak of war in 1939. In this view two of her three triple 4in mounts can be seen on her after superstructure. While primarily surface gunnery weapons, these in theory had a limited anti-aircraft capability. In practice they were ineffective in both roles.

Japanese minefield to the west of the Anamba Islands, but he rightly suspected that the enemy would also support this with a submarine patrol line, which he hoped to avoid by passing to the east of the Anamba archipelago.

However, just in case, at dawn he ordered Force Z to steer a zig-zag course, while maintaining the same economical speed of 17.5 knots. This was fast enough to outstrip any Japanese submarine, while the zig-zagging would reduce the chances of being hit by a torpedo if they did happen to come within range of one. As it had since leaving Singapore, the destroyer *Electra* led the way, sweeping for mines. None though were encountered. At 0621hrs there was a moment of tension as the destroyer *Vampire* reported spotting an unidentified aircraft to the south-east, before it disappeared into the clouds. Phillips had to weigh up the possibility that his force had been detected. However, with only a brief sighting, and no noticeable radio traffic in the area, he rightly decided that even if it was a Japanese reconnaissance plane, they hadn't been seen. Sure enough, the Japanese never reported any sighting that morning.

At 0713hrs, Force Z had reached a point 20 miles to the east of the archipelago, and Phillips ordered a turn to port, onto a new base course of 330 deg. That meant they were heading directly towards the Gulf of Siam. They also maintained their zig-zag course, while their speed remained the same. At dawn the British warships had closed up to Action Stations but now, with no visible threat, the level of readiness was stepped down, and the hands were sent to breakfast. The rest of the morning passed without incident, as the Anamba Islands slipped away astern of them. However, the islands themselves were hidden by the mist and rain.

The only break to the routine came at 0906hrs, when Captain Tennant of the *Repulse* sent Admiral Phillips a message by signal lamp. Essentially it suggested flying off one of the battlecruiser's Supermarine Walrus float planes as a scout, and detaching the destroyer *Tenedos*, which would soon be running short of fuel. It could then, Tennant suggested, help 'sweep us home' after the attack the following morning. Tennant waited for more than two hours for a reply, and when it came it merely said that a 'policy signal' would follow shortly. In other words, Phillips had already discussed his intentions before they sailed, and would pass on any changes to them when he was ready, and not before. The problem of *Tenedos*, though, prompted some signal lamp discussion of the possibility of refuelling the destroyers at sea from *Repulse*. In the end, Phillips decided not to, as this would mean reducing speed, which in turn might put their planned dawn attack in jeopardy.

At 1147hrs, Phillips ordered a slight change of direction, onto a new more northerly course of 345 deg. The intention was to keep away from a direct approach towards the beachheads. Instead, Phillips planned to keep further to the east, away from the most likely approaches to the landing areas. That would be where the Japanese would concentrate their search efforts. Then, after dark, he could alter course, and fall on the enemy from the east. Just after noon, the promised Catalina flying boat arrived from Singapore, and did a pass over the flagship. As she did so, she sent a message using her signal lamp. It said, 'Japanese making landings north of Singora.' This wasn't really fresh news – Singora in Siam (now Songkhla in Thailand) was 130 land miles (200km) up the coast from Kota Bharu. Phillips was already aware that the Japanese were landing troops in this area – all the message did was to confirm their location and Phillips intended to head towards the coast there anyway.

Then the Catalina made off into the mist ahead of them, doing her best to search for Japanese submarines or surface ships. Given the low cloud and mist, though, the chances of spotting anything from the air were slim. At 1300hrs the staff navigator announced that they were halfway to their destination. Clearly a lot depended on whether they could remain undetected, and on the situation developing along the coast of Malaya and Siam. Phillips also had other decisions to make, concerning what to do about his destroyers and their dwindling fuel stocks, and the best way to approach the enemy. For the moment, everything seemed to be going to plan. That, however, was about to change.

Admiral Phillips intended to recall the three old destroyers in Hong Kong to Singapore, to join Force Z. However, the Japanese attacked Hong Kong before the orders were given, and so the S-class destroyer *Thracian*, pictured here, had to be scuttled.

At approximately 1345hrs, Force Z was due north of the Anamba Islands, and immediately to the east of the patrol line of Japanese submarines, stationed behind the minefield. On the far eastern end of this line was I-65, an elderly Kaidai-5-class submarine commanded by Lieutenant-Commander Hakue Harada. She was actually the flagship of Submarine Division 30 (30th Submarine Flotilla), and the division's commander, Captain Maseo Teraoka, was on board the boat. On 5 December the boat sailed from Sanya on the Chinese island of Hainan, bound for her patrol area east of Terengganu on the Malayan coast. She was submerged that afternoon, and both senior officers were off duty, while the officer-of-the-watch manned the boat's control room. When he called with a sighting report, both Teraoka and Harada arrived and peered through the periscope to see it for themselves. Through the mist to the east, they could just make out the faint outline of two large warships – capital ships.

Teraoka thought one was a battlecruiser and the other a modern battleship, but in the end, at 1415hrs the following message was transmitted: 'Two Repulse type enemy battleships spotted.' It then gave their position, course and estimated speed. Unknown to Admiral Phillips, Force Z had been spotted. At the time, the British ships were probably about six miles away to the east – another mile further away and they would have been completely hidden by the mist. As it was, I-65 did not spot the four accompanying destroyers. The sighting was a major stroke of luck on the part of the Japanese. However, for various reasons it would take the best part of two hours before the sighting report was eventually passed on to Vice-Admiral Ozawa, who commanded the Japanese naval forces during the Malaya operation. Meanwhile, Force Z continued on its way, blithely unaware that the enemy now knew where they were.

The position I-65 gave in the Japanese Navy's grid reference system was Ko. Chi. SA11. This worked out at approximately 5Deg North, 105Deg 30Min East. By projecting the reported course of 340 deg for the British ships, and their reported speed of 14 knots, it was clear they were heading for the Gulf of Siam. Unfortunately for the Japanese, transmission problems on board the boat meant that it was some time before the coded message was picked up by the light cruiser *Yura*, the flagship of Rear-Admiral Daigo Taidashigi, who was in command of the fleet's submarines in the theatre. It was also received by another light cruiser, the *Kinu*, and by the 81st Naval Communications Unit, which was based in Saigon. It then took almost 90 minutes to decode, and then pass on to Vice-Admiral Jisaburo Ozawa on board his flagship, the heavy cruiser *Chokai*. It was almost 1545hrs when the admiral was handed the decoded message. In that time since the first sighting, Force Z had steamed over 40 miles closer to its objective.

The Japanese search

After the sighting, I-65 surfaced, and after speeding up to 20 knots it shadowed the British task force. However, Force Z was soon hidden by a rain squall, and although it re-appeared, the British ships were eventually swallowed up by the mist. Lieutenant-Commander Harada kept pursuing them, but at around 1700hrs the sudden appearance of an aircraft forced him to crash dive. He was worried it was a British float plane, but in fact the aircraft was a friendly one – the Kawanishi E7K float plane launched by the cruiser *Kinu*. Half an hour later, when the submarine surfaced again, the British ships were nowhere to be seen. That meant it was now up to Japanese aircraft to re-locate the British naval force. Thanks to Harada, they had a rough idea where to look, if they could find the enemy ships in the murk. There was also the chance that the British had changed course, and the search had to cover that possibility too.

The news came as a shock to Vice-Admiral Ozawa. That morning, a high-flying reconnaissance flight over Singapore had reported that *Repulse* and *Prince of Wales* were still in the naval base. Ozawa would have felt confident that the British had missed their chance to harass his landing operations. Even if they had put to sea that afternoon, the transports would be safely out of reach. As the Japanese official history put it, 'At this moment only a small amount of resupplying was continuing. Even if the British attacked from now onwards, there would be no damage done to the military units already landed… any damage would be to empty ships and a small amount of supplies. In other words, the British naval force had lost their best chance'. While this suggested that for the Japanese the critical moment had passed, this version of events was rather disingenuous.

For a start, the transport ships themselves were a finite and precious commodity. At that moment, they were protected by relatively light surface warships, and by land-based aircraft. The sighting of Force Z meant that there was now a real possibility that Admiral Phillips' two capital ships could brush aside the escorts, and wreak havoc among the transport ships. The only two Japanese battleships within range would not arrive in the area until the following morning, by which time it might be too late. Certainly it was true that the Japanese military units in Malaya were travelling light, and could effectively live off the land, but they still needed ammunition and so, without naval support, after the initial clashes they would be placed at a real disadvantage. The British, after all, had their major supply depot behind them.

Japanese ground crew manhandling a Type 96 aerial torpedo beneath a Mitsubishi Type 1 G4M bomber. When these weapons were carried, the bomber had to have its bomb doors removed, and the torpedo was slung inside the open bomb bay.

At noon on 9 December, or shortly afterwards, Ozawa had ordered the transport ships not still engaged in unloading supplies to raise anchor and put to sea. Therefore, when the news from I-65 reached him, the bulk of his transport fleet and escorts were actually heading east, bound for Cam Ranh Bay. Certainly, they were largely empty of troops and supplies, but their loss would have placed the whole Japanese plan into jeopardy. After all, once they reached Indochina they would be used in a second amphibious operation – the invasion of Borneo. This meant that when the news reached him the bulk of his detached naval units were fortuitously heading towards the area where his cruisers were operating. That would make the task of gathering together an ad hoc force of cruisers and destroyers a little easier.

Still, the news meant that Ozawa faced an operational situation which had just been turned on its head. His first task was to determine the accuracy of the sighting report. That meant confirming that the British capital ships had actually left Singapore, so he ordered an immediate photographic reconnaissance of the British naval base. When the aircraft returned to Saigon the photographs showed the two capital ships had gone. Presumably, the crew of the previous high-flying reconnaissance plane had mistaken cruisers or a floating dock for the *Repulse* and *Prince of Wales*. This confirmed they were at sea, and suggested that I-65's sighting was almost certainly genuine, but Osaka had not waited for confirmation. The sighting report from I-65 was simply too important to ignore until it could be verified.

So, when the message was forwarded to Osaka on board his flagship *Chokai*, he would have studied the chart while his staff navigator plotted the approximate whereabouts of Force Z, and the direction in which it was heading. By his reckoning it was now roughly 120 miles to the south of Osaka's covering force of cruisers. Accompanying the flagship were the four Mogami-class light cruisers *Mogami*, *Mikuma*, *Suzuya* and *Kumano*. Together they made up the 7th Cruiser Division. Each of them carried float planes, and these were ordered to be launched, and sent south in search of the enemy. At the same time Osaka ordered all remaining destroyers and cruisers to concentrate on his position, many of which were escorting the amphibious force. If he had to take on two enemy battleships, then he would need all the firepower he could get.

Further to the north-east, near the Indochina island of Con Son, was Vice-Admiral Nobutake Kondo with two battleships, the *Kongo* and *Haruna*, as well as two cruisers of the 4th Cruiser Division – *Atago* and *Takao*, accompanied by eight destroyers. They were there to provide distant cover for the landing operations. In the event of a naval battle, they would be in a position to support Osaka soon after dawn the following day. Finally, there was the transport ships themselves to consider. After the completion of the Malaya landings, they were to head back to Cam Ranh Bay near Saigon, to embark a fresh wave of troops earmarked for the invasion of Borneo. Instead, Osaka ordered them to stop unloading supplies and troops. Instead they were to scatter, heading north, deep into the Gulf of Siam. That would place them safely out of the reach of the British.

In Saigon, Rear-Admiral Matsunaga was aware of the situation, as it was his reconnaissance aircraft which had confirmed the British ships had sailed. This actually placed him in a difficult situation of his own. That morning, when that high-level reconnaissance flight suggested both capital ships were still at Singapore, he and his staff began planning an attack of their own. Matsunaga held a planning meeting to discuss whether a large-scale bombing raid could be launched against Singapore Naval Base. In effect, he wanted to repeat the success of Pearl Harbor, albeit on a smaller scale. That morning, the admiral's staff busied themselves planning the attack, and organising the waves of aircraft which would take part in it. Given the shallowness of the harbour, most of the participating Mitsubishi Type 1 G4M and Type 96 G3M were to be armed with bombs rather than torpedoes. In all, a total of 126 bombers were earmarked for the attack.

However, it was found that the two British capital ships were at sea. Matsunaga and his men now had to prepare for a completely different kind of attack. This meant that, in most

The air crews of a Japanese naval squadron of Mitsubishi Type 96 G3M2 bombers seen scrambling to their aircraft. The ability of Rear-Admiral Matsunaga's air flotilla to launch massed air attacks at short notice was the deciding factor in this short campaign.

cases, the bombs had to be removed and replaced with aerial torpedoes. First, though, as I-65 had lost contact, Force Z had to be located again. To this end, and on his own initiative, Matsunaga ordered his squadrons to join in the search for the British ships. Then, once they were located, they would be attacked by bombers equipped with torpedoes. The first four search planes were sent aloft almost immediately, at around 1650hrs. Meanwhile, on their airfields, the Japanese ground crews raced to prepare the bombers. Matsunaga knew that as sunset was at 1809hrs, there wouldn't be much time to find the enemy force, and attack it. Still, he gave the order to prepare a strike, hoping that the British ships could somehow be detected in time for the bombers to be guided to their target.

In the end, a total of 53 bombers of the Genzan and Kanoya *Kokutai* left their airfields around Singapore shortly before 1730hrs. Of these, all but nine of them carried Type 91 torpedoes, one per aircraft. The remainder were each armed with a pair of 250kg semi-armour-piercing bombs. As the estimated position of Force Z was approximately 300 miles to the south-west, it would take them just under two hours to reach the area, by which time it would be completely dark, but Matsunaga's planners knew that at 2238hrs that evening the moon would have risen sufficiently to give the bombers some chance of locating their target. He was pinning his hopes on an accurate sighting of Force Z, and then the search planes being able to vector his bombers onto their target when there was enough moonlight for the airmen to see the ships.

Without this combination of timing and moonlight, even with an accurate sighting of the enemy, it was unlikely the bombers could successfully carry out a night attack. However, at 1645hrs the mist cloaking Force Z began to dissipate. The low clouds began to disappear too. Within half an hour the skies were clear, and the low-lying sun was clearly visible. That meant the British warships would be too. On board the British ships, Admiral Phillips and his men were blithely unaware that the Japanese had spotted them earlier and that they had a rough idea where the British capital ships were, and where they were headed. Phillips was equally unaware that his opponents were mounting a large-scale search for his ships during the last hours before sunset. In fact, on board the *Prince of Wales*, the admiral's day had been taken up with the planning of the operation that lay ahead. In a series of messages sent by signal lamp, the admiral outlined the current situation and his intentions for the following day. These are worthy of repeating in their entirety. The first read as follows:

1. Besides a minor landing at Khota Bharu [sic] which was not followed up, landings have been made between Patani and Singora, and a major landing 90 miles north of Singora.
2. Little is known of enemy forces in the vicinity. It is believed that *Kongo* is the only capital ship likely to be met. Three Atago type, one Kako type, and two Zintu type cruisers have been reported. A number of destroyers, possibly of fleet type, are likely to be met.
3. My object is to surprise and sink transports and enemy warships before air attack can develop. Objective chosen will depend on air reconnaissance. Intend to arrive objective after sunrise tomorrow (10th). If an opportunity to bring *Kongo* to action occurs, this is to take precedence over all other action.
4. Subject to COs freedom of manoeuvre in an emergency, Force Z will remain in close order, and will be manoeuvred as a unit until action is joined. When the signal 'Act Independently' is made or at discretion of CO, *Repulse* will assume freedom manoeuvre, remaining in tactical support but engaging from a wide enough angle to facilitate fall of shot.
5. Intend to operate at 25 knots unless a chase develops, and subsequently to retire at maximum speed endurance will allow.
6. Capital ships should attempt to close below 20,000 yards until fire is effective, but should avoid offering an end-on target. Ships must be prepared to change from delay to non-delay fuzes according to target.
7. *Prince of Wales* and *Repulse* are each to have one aircraft fuelled and ready to fly off if required. If flown off, aircraft must return to land base. Kota Bharu aerodrome is understood to be out of action.
8. *Tenedos* will be detached before dark to return independently to Singapore.
9. Remaining destroyers may be dispatched during the night 9th/10th should enemy information require a high-speed of advance. These destroyers are to retire towards Anamba Islands at 10 knots unless a rendezvous is ordered by W/T.

This indicated two changes to the original plan. First, Admiral Phillips had taken on board Captain Tennant's suggestion of detaching *Tenedos* before her fuel reserves became critically low. The aged destroyer could then head south to the rendezvous and await further instructions. Phillips also gave her commander instructions to send a message to Singapore at 0800hrs, requesting additional destroyers put out from the naval base to meet them at the rendezvous point off the Anamba Islands. Then they could serve as an anti-submarine, minesweeping and anti-aircraft screen during the final leg of the journey back to Singapore. It also showed that Phillips was considering carrying out the attack with his two capital ships, after detaching the more vulnerable destroyers. But above all, it clearly demonstrated that Phillips expected a gunnery action, and in fact was actively seeking it.

Over the next hour, the flagship's signal lamps winked again, as other explanatory messages or additional instructions followed. First, Phillips sent one to all ships, but instead of being directed at their captains, this was aimed at their ships companies. Essentially it repeated the briefing he sent to the captains, but went out of its way to explain the strategic situation as clearly as possible: 'The enemy has made several landings on the coast of Malaya, and has made local progress. Our army is not large, and is hard-pressed in places. Our air force has had to destroy and abandon one or more aerodromes, while fat transports lie off the coast. This is our opportunity before the enemy can establish himself.' Then, Phillips outlined his plan – to surprise the enemy shortly after sunrise, and then to escape to seaward before the Japanese could react. He finished by saying, 'So, shoot to sink!'

This meant that everyone on Force Z was aware of the plan, and the reasons behind the coming attack. To them it appeared that the admiral was confident, and that they were expecting to take the enemy by surprise. In his message, Phillips had mentioned the possibility of a gun duel with the *Kongo*, or with Japanese cruisers and destroyers. He made no mention of the Japanese air threat. Next, he sent a rather needless message to the captains of both *Prince of Wales* and *Repulse*, reminding them that the crew should observe anti-flash precautions, and dress appropriately. Both captains were experienced enough not to need to be told such things. Then, in his penultimate message, sent around 1725hrs, Admiral Phillips outlined his orders for the night. It was sent to all six ships in the force: 'Course will be altered to 320° at 18.00 by signal. Course to be altered to 280° at 19.30, and speed increased to 24 knots without signal. At 22.00, destroyers are to part company without signal, and proceed to south-eastward, subsequently adjusting course and speed so as to R/V [rendezvous] at Point C at 16.00/10, unless otherwise ordered.'

Point C was 30 miles to the east of the Anamba Islands, so the dawn attack would be carried out purely by *Prince of Wales* and *Repulse*. Then, once it was over, the two capital ships would speed away to join the destroyers at the rendezvous at 1600hrs the following day. This was followed by a final message, addressed to Captain Tennant of the *Repulse*. It read, 'Unless further information is received, intend to make Singora at 07.45, and subsequently work to eastwards along coast.' The plan was made, and now everyone knew the part they had to play.

All this time the sun was creeping lower. Soon it would set, and they would be hidden from the Japanese. Suddenly, at 1745hrs, *Prince of Wales*' radar office contacted the bridge to report three small air contacts approaching them from the north. In theory her Type 279 air warning radar could easily detect approaching aircraft up to 16 miles away. That bought them sufficient time for the lookouts to search in the right direction, and the anti-aircraft gunners to prepare themselves. The lookouts spotted them – three dark specks, which were soon identified as Japanese float planes. This meant they had probably been launched from Japanese cruisers, somewhere to the north and north-west of them. In fact, they were all Aichi E13A float planes, launched from the light cruiser *Kinu* and the heavy cruisers *Kumano* and *Suzuya*. At that moment, Admiral Phillips' hopes of remaining undetected until sunset were dashed.

The *Prince of Wales*, photographed as she entered Cape Town in South Africa during her long voyage from Britain to Singapore. During her two-day stay there, the South African Prime Minister tried to warn Admiral Phillips of the threat posed by Japanese air power.

The battlecruiser *Repulse* in May 1939, pictured lying alongside Admiralty Tower in Portsmouth Dockyard. The ship was about to carry the king to Canada. The masts of the *Victory* can be seen behind her, in the same berth she occupies today.

The three float planes kept out of range of the British guns – the best their crews could do was to track them, and pray that they might drift into range. The flagship's 5.25in guns had a maximum range of 21,400m (23,400 yards), which was roughly twice that of the 4in guns mounted in *Repulse*. As a surgeon on *Prince of Wales* recalled, 'We stood on the upper deck and watched the Jap float planes in the now fading light. Our 5.25-in. guns traversed silently and menacingly, but the range was too great, and alas we had no fighter aircraft available… and we cursed the fact that sheer chance had revealed us in that short, clear period before darkness fell.' He was right – if a combat air patrol of land-based Buffalos had been there, they could have driven off or shot down the float planes before they came within sighting range of Force Z. Instead, the float planes remained unchallenged.

The aircraft from *Kinu* was the first to send off her sighting report, at 1755hrs: 'Found two enemy battleships. Position WSM, course 340°, speed 13 knots. Three escorting destroyers.' This initial report was followed by others from the remaining two float planes, which were operating a few miles to the east. Several other float planes were also aloft that evening, either from Vice-Admiral Ozawa's cruiser force or from detached warships like the *Kinu*. This in itself was a risk as, with darkness approaching, all these planes needed to find their way home. In the darkness several of them never did – one from the *Kumano* was lost at sea, one from the *Yura* crash-landed on an island and another from the *Suzuya* landed in the sea, but the plane and her three-man crew were recovered by the destroyer *Hamakaze*. The deed, however, was done. Even though the three sighting reports conflicted, the general gist remained the same – Force Z had been re-located.

While this was a relief to Ozawa, it also raised the possibility that the two forces might encounter each other in the dark. After all, the sighting report placed the British less than 30 miles to the south. With four heavy cruisers, a light cruiser and four destroyers, Ozawa knew he was outgunned. Still, his crews were extensively trained in night combat, which went some way to counteract the British use of radar-directed gunnery. However, the admiral soon had other things to worry about. While this was all taking place, the bombers from Saigon had been heading in the general direction of Force Z. Their airfields had intercepted the sighting reports from the scout planes, so their crews knew roughly where to look, but visibility was poor, as the sun had already set, and the blanket of low cloud had returned.

One of the flight commanders was Lieutenant Sadao Takai, who described what happened next: 'We did not know the definite location of the enemy warships. Furthermore, we had no information as to the location of our own ships this night. How were we to distinguish one from another?' Takai and his companions found that they could not see anything unless they flew below 300m (1,000ft). Even then, the darkness meant they had to fly over the ships or their wakes before they'd be able to spot anything in the gathering darkness. Then, as he described it, 'A radio report from one of our searching bombers brought jubilation to our ears. The anxiously sought enemy vessels had been sighted! The radio report continued: "We have dropped a flare".' The trouble was, it was dropped over the wrong ship. Instead of the *Prince of Wales* or *Repulse*, the flare had landed next to Vice-Admiral Ozawa's flagship, the *Chokai*.

Ozawa immediately sent an emergency signal to Matsunaga in Saigon, sent uncoded, which said simply, 'There are three attacking planes above *Chokai*. It is *Chokai* under the flare!' At the same time, he ordered his ships to turn away towards the north, to get away from the flare, and to reduce the risk of being bombed. However, back in Saigon, when Rear-Admiral Matsunaga read the signal he realised that he needed to abort the whole operation. After all, the conditions over the Gulf of Siam were too poor to easily identify Force Z if it were found, and the mistaking of the *Chokai* for a British ship showed that conditions simply weren't suitable. He could wait until the moon rose, but by then the bombers would be running low on fuel, so it made much more sense to recall the bombers, and hope for more favourable conditions the following morning.

Two other factors influenced Matsunaga's decision. First, there were only 78 aerial torpedoes available in his airfields. This effectively meant one per bomber, so there was no room for speculative attacks – every torpedo had to count. This in itself rendered a night attack prohibitively wasteful. It made far more sense to wait until daylight, when the air crews would have a better chance of carrying out an effective torpedo run. The other was Vice-Admiral Kondo, currently at sea in the battleship *Kongo*. Having intercepted the *Chokai* signal, he realised that a night attack by bombers and a night battle by surface warships were both fraught with danger. Here would be no guarantee of a favourable result. Kondo therefore approved Matsunaga's decision to recall his bombers, but he also ordered Ozawa to avoid engaging the enemy until dawn the following day, to give his force more time to gather, and to fully prepare the crews for what lay ahead.

This night battle was even closer than either Kondo or Ozawa imagined. When the reconnaissance bomber dropped its flare next to the *Chokai*, the glow was spotted by lookouts on board the British destroyer *Electra*. The time was 1856hrs. For the British, this came at the end of a busy hour. First, just before sunset the lookouts noted the return of the low cloud. This, combined with the growing darkness should help screen them from any more attention by Japanese aircraft. Their original three shadowers, though, had been seen to head away towards the north, their progress followed by the flagship's radar. At 1839hrs, following Admiral Phillips' instructions, the destroyer *Tenedos* peeled away from the formation, and set a course towards the south. That left Force Z with just three destroyers. Then, at 1850hrs, again in accordance with Phillips' instructions, the force altered course to port, onto a new course of 320 deg. They also increased their speed to 26 knots.

The British warships had barely settled onto their new course when *Electra*'s lookouts spotted the flare off their starboard bow. The destroyer was on the starboard beam of the British force, which was now heading towards the north-west. The same lookouts estimated that the flare, seen dropping through the low clouds, was illuminating a spot roughly five miles to the north-north-west of them. The news was immediately flashed by signal lamp to the flagship. On board the *Prince of Wales*, Phillips decided to err on the side of caution. He ordered a course change to port, onto a new heading of 230 deg. That meant they were now heading at right angles to their previous course, away from the flare. Phillips wasn't sure what had set it off, but rightly concluded that it indicated the presence of enemy surface ships.

Although this air attack took place off Guadalcanal in August 1942, it shows what the attack on Force Z would have looked like, if a similar scene had been recorded. Here, Type 1 bombers launch low-level torpedo attacks on American warships.

Now, with Ozawa heading north and Phillips to the south-west, the two groups of ships were heading away from each other. It was surprising that the *Chokai* and her consorts hadn't been picked up on radar. After all, the Type 279 radar on the *Prince of Wales* should have been able to detect a contact the size of an enemy cruiser at a range of 20 miles. However, radar was an imprecise tool, and dependent on atmospheric conditions. Therefore, both forces turned away without sighting the enemy. It is interesting to speculate what might have happened if the two sides had clashed that evening, but the opportunity quickly passed. Instead, on the British flagship, Admiral Phillips had his own decision to make – the toughest of his life. It didn't just affect Force Z – it could also determine the very future of the British Empire.

Manoeuvres in the night

By now it was clear that Force Z couldn't go ahead with its mission. The Japanese knew where they were, and would fully understand the threat to the landing operations. Therefore, Phillips expected that his Japanese counterparts would move the transports out of reach of the British ships. That meant that he could no longer expect to inflict havoc on them at dawn. Instead, he predicted that the Japanese would gather all their available surface warships into a task force capable of taking on the British capital ships. His latest intelligence report, sent by Rear-Admiral Palliser that evening, suggested that he could expect this to consist of a minimum of 'one battleship, one M class [Mogami-class] cruiser and 11 destroyers'. That was the Japanese force reported off Kota Bharu that morning. Furthermore, he expected additional cruisers and destroyers to be operating as screening forces.

The prospect of a naval clash at dawn did not worry Phillips. In fact, he had been hoping to bring the Japanese to battle since his arrival in Far Eastern waters. However, he also understood that to continue with his mission, even after all chance of achieving its primary objective had faded, was not a viable option. He would merely be placing his two capital ships at risk. He also expected that, after the sighting, all available Japanese submarines would most likely be heading towards them through the night. That meant that Force Z was at a much-heightened risk from torpedoes. Finally, there was the air component of the battle. At dawn the Japanese would also send out more search aircraft, followed by land-based bombers. His chances of obtaining friendly air cover from the beleaguered RAF were minimal.

To continue deeper into the Gulf of Siam would achieve little. Instead, it would needlessly place Force Z in grave danger. There was no real option left – he had to call off the operation. At 2005hrs he ordered a reduction in speed to 20 knots. Then, at 2020hrs, he ordered a change of course, turning the task force to port, onto a heading of 150 deg. Half an hour later, at 2050hrs, he ordered the following signal to be flashed to all his remaining ships: 'I have most regretfully cancelled the operation because, having been located by aircraft, surprise was lost, and our target would be almost certain to be gone by the morning, and the enemy fully prepared for us.' The signal was duly acknowledged by *Repulse* and the three remaining destroyers, followed by a signal from Captain Tennant, supporting Phillips' difficult decision. Force Z began their long journey back to Singapore.

From that point on, Force Z was heading out of danger. At their current course and speed, Phillips could expect them to be 170 miles further south by dawn. That should, in theory, place them some 50 miles to the north-east of the Anamba Islands, and close to their planned rendezvous with their destroyers, if they had actually been detached. However, they were not out of danger yet. While the Japanese naval forces of Vice-Admirals Kondo and Ozawa were now too far away to successfully bring Force Z to battle, the waters between them and the island archipelago were infested with Japanese submarines. Also, with the range to reach Singapore if required, the Japanese bombers based around Saigon could still attack them, if the British force could be located. For Phillips it was a worrying evening, but at least he had made his decision, and so his ships had a good chance of extricating themselves.

Meanwhile, back in Singapore, Rear-Admiral Palliser continued to act as a conduit for information. While Phillips was maintaining strict radio silence, to avoid betraying his position, his subordinate was free to update the admiral on any important developments. At 2145hrs, almost an hour after Phillips officially cancelled the operation, his evening radio message reached the flagship. Palliser reported that the enemy were continuing landing operations at both Kota Bharu and Singora, but the RAF was under considerable pressure, and Kota Bharu airfield had been overrun. Given that Phillips had cancelled the operation, this information was no longer relevant. However, in his signal, Palliser added his latest information on the Japanese bomber force: 'Enemy bombers on South Indochina aerodromes are in force and undisturbed. They could attack you five hours after sighting, and much depends on whether you have been seen today.'

The hope that the Americans would suppress the Japanese airfields around Saigon had been unfulfilled. That meant they still had the bomber capacity to attack Force Z during its voyage back to Singapore. Palliser had no idea that Force Z had already been sighted, and of course he had only the vaguest idea where it was that evening. In his signal he added another warning that, 'Two carriers may be in Saigon area.' This was the result of a misidentified sighting by American aircraft. The two vessels were actually the seaplane tenders *Chitose* and *Chiyoda*, earmarked to support the Borneo operation. While this might have been based on incorrect intelligence, the air threat from Saigon was real enough. While Admiral Phillips may have been inclined to underplay the potential danger of an attack by land-based bombers, his deputy seems to have considered it a real risk.

As a battlecruiser rather than a battleship, the design of *Repulse* emphasised speed and firepower rather than protection. Beneath her thin armoured belt she was protected by just 5.1cm (2in) of steel, although she was also fitted with anti-torpedo bulges, to absorb some of a torpedo's impact.

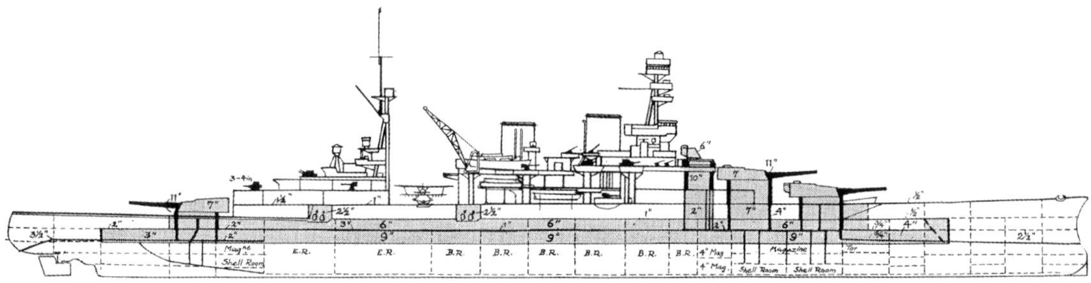

Then, at 2352hrs, Palliser sent another brief signal – one that would turn the whole situation on its head. It read, 'Immediate. Enemy reported landing Kuantan, Latitude 03.50 North.' Kuantan was a small port on Malaya's eastern coast, roughly midway between Kota Bharu and Singapore. If the report were true, then the Japanese could well cut off most of the Commonwealth troops to the north. It had all the hallmarks of a disaster in the making. While we aren't privy to Admiral Phillips' thoughts that night, he must have worked out the importance of the news for himself. Kuantan was 180 miles to the south-east of Force Z's current position. That meant that at 25 knots, Force Z could be off the port around 0800hrs the following morning. The Japanese might have spotted him the previous evening, but they would expect him to be far to the north, or else on his way back to Singapore. With luck, a dawn attack off Kuantan might give him a real chance to make a difference.

Just after midnight, Phillips gave the order and the flagship's blue night signal lamp began flashing again. This time they altered course 90 deg to starboard, onto a new course of 240 deg. He also increased speed to 25 knots. His staff navigator estimated that they would be within gun range of the landing beaches shortly after 0700hrs, so the admiral planned to fly off a Walrus float plane shortly before they made landfall, to conduct a sweep of the landing area, and then to help direct the capital ships' guns. This makeshift plan was now in place. Phillips would have preferred to have air cover over his ships as he approached Kuantan, but to request that would mean breaking radio silence – something he was not prepared to do. That way the Japanese would be taken by surprise.

However, the British admiral didn't know it, but Force Z had already been detected by the Japanese. Shortly before midnight, at 2352hrs, bridge lookouts on the submarine I-58 spotted the silhouettes of two large warships, fine off their starboard bow. The boat was on the surface at the time, so her commander, Lieutenant-Commander Sohichi Kitamura ordered her to crash dive. At the same time, he sent off a brief sighting report, but it was not picked up and passed on. When he dived, Kitamura estimated the warships were just 600m (660 yards) away. Once safely beneath the surface, Kitamura raised his periscope and had a look. He quickly identified the vessels as the two British capital ships his whole flotilla had been searching for. The leading ship was the *Prince of Wales*, followed by the *Repulse*, escorted by three destroyers, passing him from left to right, and at a perfect range and angle for a torpedo attack.

However, as the tubes were made ready one of the torpedo hatches jammed. By the time the problem was dealt with the two capital ships had passed them by, and he no longer had a decent shot at them. Still, he launched five torpedoes at the *Repulse*, which at the time was heading away from him towards the south. All five torpedoes missed. It appears that nobody in Force Z managed to detect the torpedoes, or the enemy submarine – Kitamura had missed his big chance. It was an incredibly frustrating moment, but at least he was not detected by the two capital ships, or the destroyers accompanying them. Once they had passed he was also able to surface again, and set off in pursuit of the enemy force, making his boat's top speed of 16 knots. He was also able to send off another longer sighting report. In it, he reported unsuccessfully launching a spread of torpedoes at *Repulse*, and gave her estimated course and speed – 180 deg and 22 knots.

Since the attack, the British had changed course towards the south-west, so Kitamura sent another signal giving the details, although by then all he could see of the enemy ships was their funnel smoke. He pursued them for a while, but at 0315hrs he sent another signal, reporting that he had lost contact. This time the second sighting report was received by Kondo, Ozawa and Matsunaga, but not the crucial third one, reporting the change of course. Therefore, while the Japanese now knew that Force Z had turned around and was heading back to Singapore, it still had no idea that Phillips had decided to launch a dawn attack on the Japanese transports off Kuantan. During the early hours of 10 December, Phillips received another signal from Palliser, relaying a message from the Admiralty.

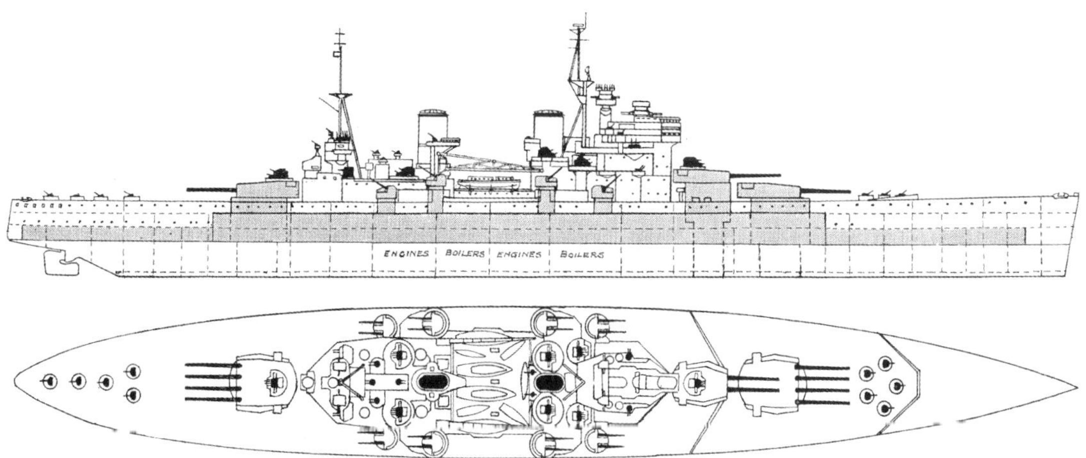

Prince of Wales was protected by a thick armour, designed to protect her turrets and 'vitals' (machinery spaces and magazines) from enemy shells. Below the waterline, though, she was less well-protected, as her armoured belt there was only 11.4cm (4.5in) thick.

It merely raised the possibility of a Japanese air attack on the naval base at Singapore, but Phillips ignored it, as his force was already at sea.

In the Gulf of Siam that morning, Wednesday 10 December, dawn broke at 0503hrs. A few minutes earlier, Phillips had reduced the force's speed to 17 knots. The crews of the British ships had already had breakfast, and were at Action Stations. They were approaching the coast, and an enemy landing area, so they had to be ready for anything. Sure enough, at 0515hrs they spotted something on the northern horizon. It turned out to be a tug towing three barges. It was assumed it was Japanese, and these were troop carriers. Presumably they were reinforcing the main landing. Still, these could wait, and so Phillips pressed on towards Kuantan. At 0630hrs a plane was spotted, and it seemed to be shadowing them. Again, it was presumed it was Japanese, but its identity remains a mystery, as no sighting reports were radioed in to the Japanese naval commanders.

They were now less than 30 miles from the coast, and so Phillips ordered the flagship's Walrus float plane to be launched, to take a look at what lay ahead, and then report back. It was launched at 0718hrs, and within 20 minutes it was over the coast at Kuantan. Its pilot, Lieutenant Clement Bateman, radioed the *Prince of Wales* to say there was no Japanese invasion lying off the small port. The seaplane then headed off to Singapore. This report was perplexing. What of Rear-Admiral Palliser's message? By 0800hrs, the coast was just within sight. Phillips sent the destroyer *Express* inshore at full speed to investigate. Half an hour later she was steaming off Kuantan, and found the town and the beaches on either side of

HMS *Repulse* under attack, late morning

Shortly before 1100hrs on 10 December, a squadron of Japanese bombers sighted Force Z, and began closing with it from the south-east. These eight Mitsubishi Type 96 bombers of 1/Mihoro *Kokutai* were armed with bombs rather than torpedoes, and so they made their approach at a steady 3,000m (9,850ft), flying in a tight line-abreast formation. The British ships opened fire at 1109hrs, but the attackers did not waver. The closest British capital ship was the *Prince of Wales*, but it soon became clear she was not the target. The bombers passed over her, and on towards the *Repulse*, which, unlike the flagship, did not try to manoeuvre. Instead, Captain Tennant ordered an increase in speed, to confuse the Japanese bomb aimers. He also did not want to throw off the aim of his anti-aircraft gunners, who managed to damage two of the approaching bombers. This last-minute burst of speed almost worked. At 1113hrs each of the bombers released a single 250kg bomb – half of their payload. Seven of them fell close to the battlecruiser, four to port and three to starboard, and all a little astern of her. However, one bomb struck *Repulse* on her hangar, and plunged through it before exploding in the deck below. Although no serious damage was done, several men were wounded, and a fire was started which irreparably damaged the ship's remaining Walrus float plane. It was a close escape, but this was merely the start of the relentless attacks. Much worse was to come.

it completely empty of shipping. There was no Japanese invasion force. By 0900hrs she had re-joined Force Z, and reputedly the destroyer's captain, Lieutenant-Commander Francis Cartwright signalled the flagship, reporting that, 'All as quiet as a wet Sunday afternoon'.

There is still some confusion over exactly what happened, but the likelihood was that the previous evening the Japanese staged a diversion around Kuantan, to draw Commonwealth troops away from the fighting to the north. The inexperienced Indian brigade stationed around the town fell for the ploy, and raised the alarm. Later, some small bullet-holed Japanese boats were found to the south of Kuantan, which suggested the whole thing had been a ruse. If so, then it was one which reaped unexpected dividends. What is surprising is that Admiral Phillips dallied off Kuantan so long after learning there was no invasion force. It was now after 0900hrs, and they had delayed leaving the area for an hour and a half after Lieutenant Bateman's report from the Walrus.

At this point, Captain Tennant of the *Repulse* signalled the flagship, with two suggestions. The first was for permission to fly off a Walrus, to conduct an anti-submarine sweep around the force. Phillips agreed, and the seaplane was launched, with orders to return to Singapore afterwards. Tennant then suggested investigating the tug and barges seen earlier. Again, Phillips agreed, and so at 0930hrs, Force Z turned away from the coast, and steered out to sea, on a new easterly course of 080 deg. The tug could have been investigated by a destroyer, but presumably Phillips thought it might merely be part of a larger force. This, however, wasn't much of a diversion, as the original intention was to head home by way of the rendezvous point off the Anamba Islands, which lay 180 miles to the east. From there they had a similar distance to go before they could reach Singapore. But what the Kuantan diversion had meant, was that they had lingered much longer than was prudent.

The danger was finally revealed half an hour later, at 1005hrs. It came in the form of a signal from the destroyer *Tenedos*, reporting she was under air attack. Her position was given as 140 miles to the south-east of Force Z, just to the north-west of the archipelago. That told Phillips two things. First, the Japanese had sent bombers aloft, and these were probably looking for him. Second, it proved that as *Tenedos* was roughly the same distance away from the airfields around Saigon as Force Z was, then they were well within range of these land-based aircraft.

This, of course, was no surprise to the admiral. After all, the Admiralty considered that even Singapore itself lay within reach of the Japanese bombers. However, it stripped away any last illusion that they were safe from attack. This was underlined six minutes later, at 1011hrs, when lookouts on *Prince of Wales* spotted a high-flying aircraft approaching them from the east. That meant it could only be Japanese. Given the attack on *Tenedos*, the likelihood was that it was a reconnaissance plane. It would radio Force Z's position, and so, inevitably, its appearance was merely the prelude to an air attack. The British were already at Action Stations, and all anti-aircraft guns manned and ready. Radar crews and lookouts were well aware of the threat, and so were being as diligent as they could be. Soon, the effectiveness of Force Z's air defences would be put to the test.

The first attack

The sighting report from the submarine I-58 sent out at 0211hrs eventually reached Rear-Admiral Matsunaga in Saigon. He quickly realised that Kondo and Ozawa's naval task forces were too far to the north to stop Force Z. Similarly, the Japanese submarine line was too far to the west to intercept the British. That meant, as he saw it, it was up to his aircraft. He immediately ordered all his available bombers to be refuelled, re-armed and readied for a mission soon after dawn. Of the 99 bombers in the three *Kokutai* under his command, 94 of them were available for the operation. This was an impressive tally, given that for the past two days the three *Kokutai* had been heavily involved in supporting the Malaya invasion,

This blurred action shot, purportedly taken from a Japanese torpedo-carrying bomber shows the first stage of the air attack on Force Z under way. The destroyer in the foreground is possibly the *Express*, with *Prince of Wales* in the middle distance.

and in the search for Force Z. In fact the last bombers from his recalled air strike from the previous evening had only just returned home. The air crews may have been exhausted, but there would be no respite for them as long as Force Z was within reach.

Originally, Matsunaga planned to use 17 of his bombers in a reconnaissance role, which left 77 aircraft available to take part in the attack. Of these, 17 would be used as traditional bombers, while the remaining 60 aircraft would carry torpedoes. At 0400hrs, though, the admiral revised this allocation. Now, just nine bombers would be used as search aircraft. Instead, they would be used as high-level bombers. Similarly, a squadron of nine more aircraft were ordered to be re-armed with bombs rather than torpedoes. That meant the total allocation of the 94 aircraft was for a total of 85 bombers, 34 armed with bombs, and 51 with torpedoes. The remaining nine aircraft would be used as the reconnaissance force. The search aircraft would take off before dawn at 0500hrs, while the bombers would begin taking off almost 90 minutes later, from 0630hrs onwards. During the early hours of Wednesday morning, therefore, the Japanese airfield bustled with activity.

The nine reconnaissance aircraft – three from each *Kokutai* were all Type 96 G3M2 bombers. They were provided with full fuel tanks, which in theory gave them an impressive range of 1,200 nautical miles, flying at 3,000m (10,000ft) and 150 knots. Before take-off the crews were briefed on their search pattern. Essentially it would form a large fan, radiating out from Saigon, in the general direction of the Anamba Islands. Once the aircraft reached the limit of their search pattern, well to the south of the islands and to the east of Singapore, they would turn and head home some distance to the west, in their neighbour's search area. Just in case they had a chance to use them, each bomber carried two 50kg semi-armour-piercing bombs. These were of little more than token use, there to boost crew morale after being relegated to what many would see as a secondary role in the operation.

Like her predecessor the Type 96, the Mitsubishi Type 1 G4M 'Betty' bomber lacked self-sealing tanks or armoured protection for her crew. This was a trade-off in order to extend the bomber's range. As a result, these aircraft were particularly vulnerable to well-directed anti-aircraft fire.

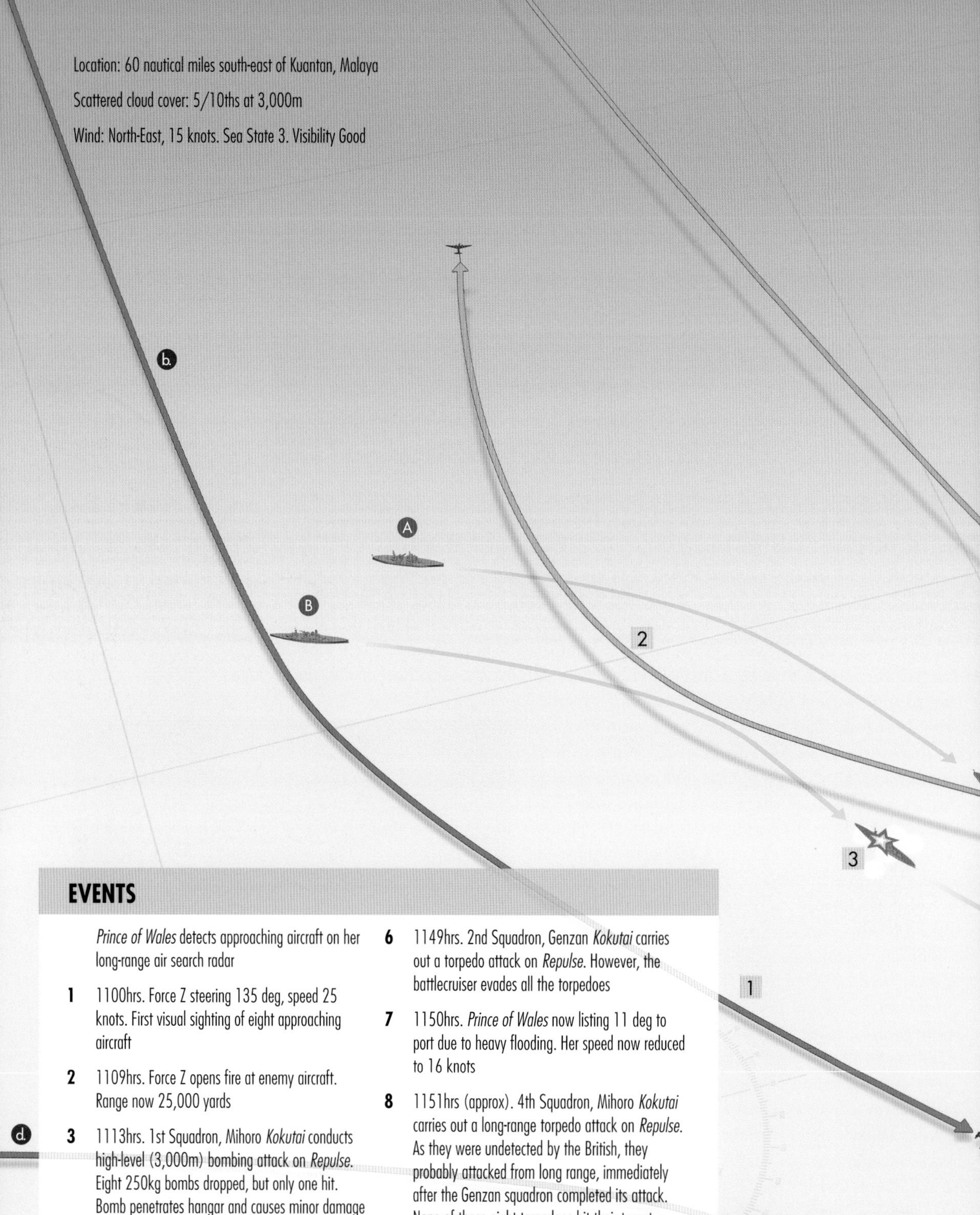

EVENTS

Prince of Wales detects approaching aircraft on her long-range air search radar

1 1100hrs. Force Z steering 135 deg, speed 25 knots. First visual sighting of eight approaching aircraft

2 1109hrs. Force Z opens fire at enemy aircraft. Range now 25,000 yards

3 1113hrs. 1st Squadron, Mihoro *Kokutai* conducts high-level (3,000m) bombing attack on *Repulse*. Eight 250kg bombs dropped, but only one hit. Bomb penetrates hangar and causes minor damage

4 1141hrs. 1st Squadron, Genzan *Kokutai* carries out low-level torpedo attack on *Prince of Wales*

5 1141hrs. *Prince of Wales* hit on her starboard quarter by a torpedo. Crippling damage to port outer propeller shaft

6 1149hrs. 2nd Squadron, Genzan *Kokutai* carries out a torpedo attack on *Repulse*. However, the battlecruiser evades all the torpedoes

7 1150hrs. *Prince of Wales* now listing 11 deg to port due to heavy flooding. Her speed now reduced to 16 knots

8 1151hrs (approx). 4th Squadron, Mihoro *Kokutai* carries out a long-range torpedo attack on *Repulse*. As they were undetected by the British, they probably attacked from long range, immediately after the Genzan squadron completed its attack. None of these eight torpedoes hit their target

9 1157hrs. 1st Squadron, Mihoro *Kokutai* returns to carry out another high-level bombing attack on *Repulse*. All six 250kg HE bombs miss

1158hrs. Flagship orders all anti-aircraft guns to cease fire

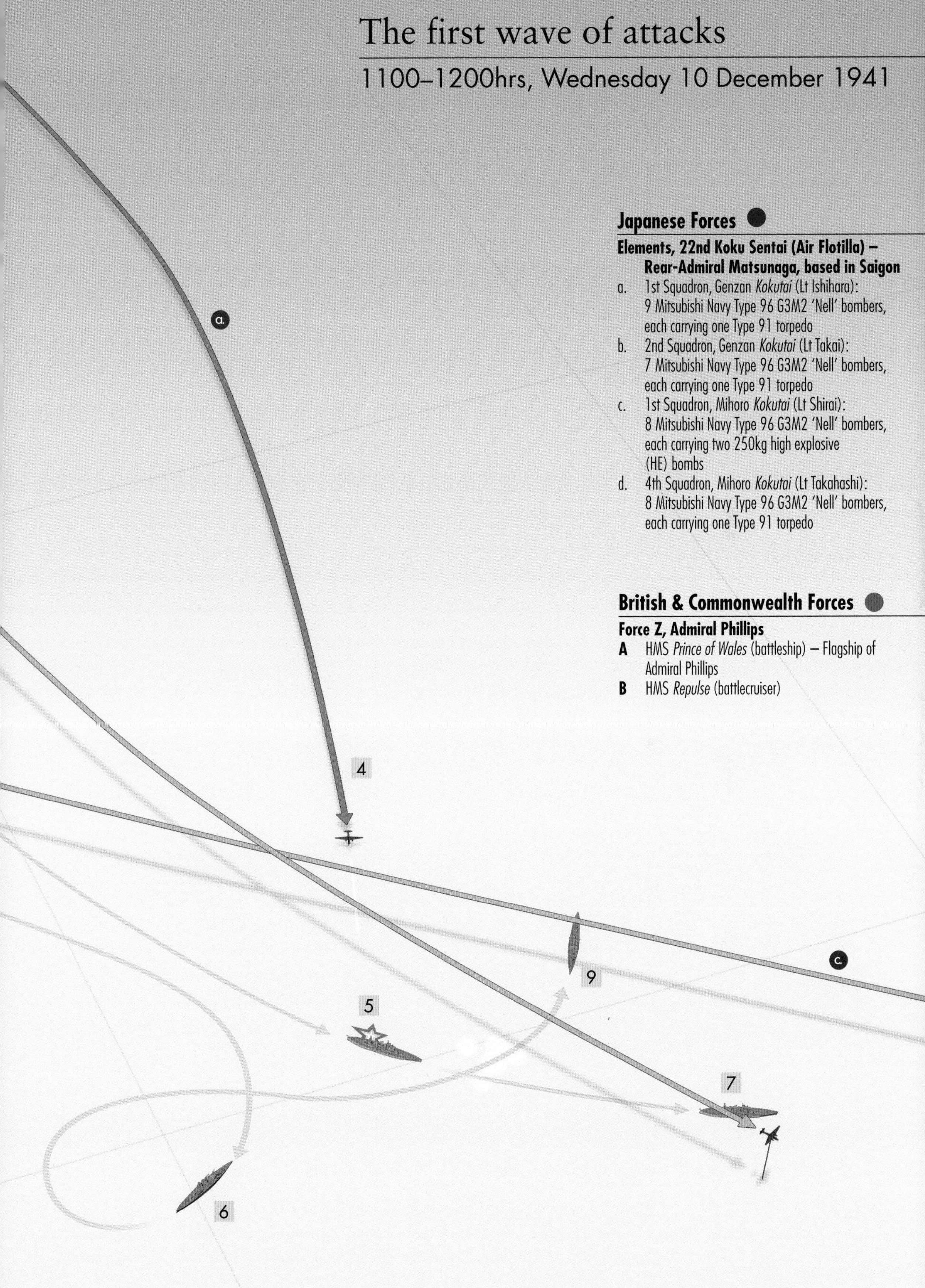
The first wave of attacks
1100–1200hrs, Wednesday 10 December 1941
Japanese Forces
Elements, 22nd Koku Sentai (Air Flotilla) – Rear-Admiral Matsunaga, based in Saigon
a. 1st Squadron, Genzan Kokutai (Lt Ishihara): 9 Mitsubishi Navy Type 96 G3M2 'Nell' bombers, each carrying one Type 91 torpedo
b. 2nd Squadron, Genzan Kokutai (Lt Takai): 7 Mitsubishi Navy Type 96 G3M2 'Nell' bombers, each carrying one Type 91 torpedo
c. 1st Squadron, Mihoro Kokutai (Lt Shirai): 8 Mitsubishi Navy Type 96 G3M2 'Nell' bombers, each carrying two 250kg high explosive (HE) bombs
d. 4th Squadron, Mihoro Kokutai (Lt Takahashi): 8 Mitsubishi Navy Type 96 G3M2 'Nell' bombers, each carrying one Type 91 torpedo
British & Commonwealth Forces
Force Z, Admiral Phillips
A HMS Prince of Wales (battleship) – Flagship of Admiral Phillips
B HMS Repulse (battlecruiser)
a.
4
c.
9
5
7
6

These nine aircraft took off on schedule at 0500hrs. By that time the ground crews were busy rearming the eight remaining reconnaissance planes with larger bombs, and compensating for this change in weight by removing some of the fuel in their tanks. While the sleepy air crews were being briefed and fed, the remaining aircraft were being made ready. It was made clear that this was a vitally important mission – the destruction of Force Z was crucial to the advancement of Japanese plans in the region. It was also very clear that, like the mission the previous evening, everything depended on the reconnaissance aircraft being able to locate the enemy ships, and then direct the bombers towards their target. Everything depended on good eyesight – and luck. Attack plans had already been established, but just in case, the crews were also briefed on the anti-aircraft potential of their targets, and tactics were adjusted accordingly.

The general idea was that the aircraft armed with bombs would attack first, approaching Force Z at high altitude. As no armour-piercing bombs were available, these bombers, all Type 96 G3M2s, were armed with either two 250kg regular bombs, or a single 500kg one. The aim was not to sink the two capital ships. Instead, it was expected that these bombs would explode on the superstructure of the target, damaging or destroying exposed anti-aircraft guns, and killing or wounding their crews. This would then make it easier for the more vulnerable torpedo bombers to make their attack. All aircraft would approach their target in squadron-sized formations of eight or nine aircraft, but the actual attacks would be made by flights of two or three bombers. The Japanese air crews had trained in high-level bombing against ships, but until now they'd never had a chance to put their skills to use.

Then, after the high-level bombing was completed, the torpedo-carrying bombers would make their runs. Again, they would make their approach in squadrons, but break into flights for their actual torpedo runs. It was also emphasised that different squadrons should attack the target from two or more directions at once, to make it much harder for the defenders to evade the torpedoes. The Modified Type 91 aerial torpedo had a range of 2,000m (2,200 yards) and a speed of 42 knots, but Japanese tactics called for its release 700–1,000m from the target. That would give it a run time of between 30 to 42 seconds. If the attack had to be made in confined waters, such as in Singapore Naval Base, then ranges would be reduced. If all went to plan, though, the bombers would catch the British ships in the open sea.

The 26 Type 96 G3M2s that made up the Genzan *Kokutai* began taking off from Saigon's Tan Son Nhat airfield just after 0625hrs. From 0644hrs on they were followed by the Kanoya *Kokutai*, with 26 Type 1 G4M1s, which took off from the nearby airfield of Dau Mot. Following them were the first 24 Type 96 bombers of the Mihoro *Kokutai*. The group's remaining squadron, the 3rd, did not leave before 0800hrs. Their departure had been delayed by their last-minute switch from torpedoes to bombs. Once the bombers reached their flying altitude of 3,000m (9,840ft) their speed was cut to around 150 knots – slightly below their usual cruising speed, to make the most of their fuel. After all, until the reconnaissance aircraft had located Force Z, these bombers did not have a target to attack, and so it made sense to conserve fuel, and so prolong the aircrafts' endurance.

While Rear-Admiral Matsunaga and his staff had no definite location to head for, it was probable that Force Z would be located within 500 nautical miles of these home airfields. This was important, as in order to compensate for their weapons payload, they had a reduced fuel load, which limited their endurance. The torpedo-carrying Type 1s of the Kanoya *Kokutai* were the worst affected, with their usual range of 1,540 nautical miles reduced by half. The older Type 96s used by the other *two Kokutai* had a longer range, and could even reach Singapore if required, but fuel consumption and capacity remained a concern. In case of emergency, the pilots were instructed to head to the freshly captured airfield at Kota Bharu, which was hurriedly being readied to accommodate them.

The hours passed, and the bombers flew southwards, preceded by the reconnaissance planes. However, the much-anticipated sighting report never came. The frustration felt by the bomber crews was voiced by Lieutenant Takai, commanding the Genzan *Kokutai*'s 2nd Squadron:

> Still no sign of the enemy. In spite of the good weather and clear visibility, is it possible the reconnaissance planes still cannot find the British warships? By now our planes should be more than 500 nautical miles from Saigon… We have passed the danger line of 400 nautical miles from Saigon… The pilots are becoming more and more anxious about their remaining fuel. We measured the rate of fuel consumption and reduced it to the lowest possible level.

He then added that one of his bombers developed engine trouble, and had to return to base. That left his squadron with seven aircraft.

By now the nine search planes had reached the southern extent of their sweep, roughly on the same latitude as the Anamba Islands. They all flew to the east for a short distance, before heading home, still searching as they went. The fourth plane in the search pattern had passed the island of Tioman before turning towards the south-east, and after 25 miles the bomber banked around to the north for its homeward leg. Then, at 0943hrs, it spotted a ship below them. The air crew identified her as a British destroyer. Rather than wasting this opportunity, the bomber banked around, and made a bombing run on her, releasing her two 50kg bombs. Both missed, overshooting the target. The sighting was reported, and the reconnaissance plane resumed its long flight home. Her signal, though, was picked up by the Genzan *Kokutai*, which was some 60 miles to the north-east. A little later, as they were on almost reciprocal courses, the search plane passed the 25 bombers, in close formation but split into its three squadrons, all flying south at 3,000m (9,840ft).

Again, Lieutenant Takai took up the story:

> At 10.15 we sighted a small vessel off to our left. The sea was absolutely calm. The ship appeared to be a cargo vessel of about five or six hundred tons. Singapore was near. Since it was possible that other enemy vessels might be in the vicinity, I ordered my men to stay alert. No other object could be seen – this was unusual. Keeping a sharp lookout above and behind us for enemy planes, we tightened all formations and maintained our flight due south.

Despite its shortcomings, two of the three Japanese bombers shot down during the attack were hit by 2-pounder shells fired from the ships' eight-barrelled 'pom-poms' – one claimed by *Repulse*, the other by *Prince of Wales*. The third casualty was hit by a 5.25in shell fired from the flagship.

In fact the ship they spotted was not a cargo ship – it was the destroyer *Tenedos*, heading home to Singapore. It was a target that should have been ignored. However, as Takai recorded, 'Without warning the entire 3rd squadron dropped out of the mass formation and flew towards the small cargo vessel.'

This certainly was not part of the plan. The commander of the 3rd squadron, Lieutenant Nikaido, had no reason to attack the lone destroyer, but he gave the order nonetheless, and the nine bombers began their bombing run. Takai watched the attack: 'Soon they circled over the ship… the enemy vessel suddenly changed its course, and no sooner had it begun its twisting, evasive action than a salvo of bombs fell'. All nine of the 500kg bombs missed, most landing over 100m off the destroyer's port beam. On board the *Tenedos*, her commander, Lieutenant Richard Dyer, handled his ship superbly – the reason Takai saw the bombers circling was because they had to make three runs before Nikaido felt confident enough to order the release of the bombs. As Dyer put it later, 'She [*Tenedos*] handled like a dream, and the almighty was with us.'

This, of course, deprived Rear-Admiral Matsunaga of an entire squadron of nine Type 96 bombers. After the attack the 3rd squadron re-formed, and with their bombs gone, the aircraft sheepishly headed back to Saigon. What was even more surprising was that in the squadron leader's bomber was a passenger – Captain Maeda, the commander of the *Kokutai*. Rather than wait back in Saigon, he had decided to see the attack on Force Z for himself. However, when the attack on the *Tenedos* began, he didn't call it off. On board the destroyer, the crew only suffered one casualty – a seaman, wounded in the thigh by a piece of shrapnel. As the destroyer continued on towards Singapore, the remaining two torpedo-carrying squadrons of the Genzan *Kokutai* continued on their original course. They at least were still in the fight.

Naturally, *Tenedos* sent off a report. Strangely, while this was received by the warships of Force Z, some 140 miles to the north-west, it was not picked up by the wireless station in Singapore, 120 miles to the south-west. Naturally, this news was viewed with some unease on board the *Prince of Wales*. In Force Z, the crews had been at Action Stations while off Kuantan, but since turning away from the coast they had been stood down, to give the crews a chance to eat a proper cooked breakfast. For many, it would be their last meal. They had been heading towards the tug and barges sighted earlier that morning, steering a course of 080 deg.

Later, Phillips ordered two course changes, first at 1000hrs to a more easterly heading of 095 deg, and then at 1005hrs, onto a course of 135 deg. This was not in response to the signal from *Tenedos*, but because a vessel was spotted to the south-east. She turned out to be a British-registered freighter, the SS *Haldis*, en route from Hong Kong to Singapore, but Phillips did not have a chance to warn her captain of the newly laid Japanese minefield ahead of him before being overtaken by a new development. In theory, the minefield lay 85 miles ahead of both the warships and the freighter, and between them and the *Tenedos*. Phillips still had the option to head around it, or even pass through it with his destroyers sweeping ahead of him, but, in all likelihood, he still considered it probable that a Japanese invasion force was somewhere in the area. By stopping it he could deal a crippling blow to the enemy, but, by remaining in the area, he was placing his warships in grave danger.

Meanwhile, Rear-Admiral Matsunaga's air crews were all well aware that they were close to their maximum range. Soon, if no sighting was made, they would have to turn around and head home. The planes of the Mihoro *Kokutai* were slightly more fortunate, as they had taken off later, and so were a little further to the north. This was particularly true of the 3rd squadron, which had taken off over an hour after the others, and so was 150 miles behind the rest of the *Kokutai*. Everything now depended on the search planes. Then, suddenly, the crew of the third of the search planes spotted something. The bomber had already reached the end of its search area, but, like its counterpart who found the *Tenedos*, it flew off at right angles for a few minutes before commencing its return leg towards Saigon. A few minutes later, they spotted a formation of warships below them. It was Force Z.

At 1015hrs, the search plane's commander, Midshipman Hoashi, sent off the first of several sighting reports. It gave the location, 4Deg North, 103Deg 55Min East, and the fact that the enemy were heading on a course of 060 deg. Incidentally, this was the same moment when the Genzan *Kokutai* were attacking the *Tenedos*. A few minutes later, Hoashi identified the enemy warships as a 'King type' battleship, the battlecruiser *Repulse* and three destroyers. He also reported a course change of 30 deg. For some reason, while these sighting reports reached Singapore, they were not received by many of the attack bombers, so the messages from the search plane had to be passed on to them by Matsunaga's headquarters. Still, the key thing was, the British force had been found.

On board the *Prince of Wales*, the search plane was spotted to the south of them, but there was nothing anyone could do, apart from wait to see what happened next. From now on, the Japanese would hold the initiative. Some mentioned a sense of foreboding as they watched the Japanese plane trailing them. What is surprising was that even at that late stage, Admiral Phillips refused to break radio silence and request air support. Had he made the request when the search plane first appeared, then there was a reasonable chance the Brewster Buffalos of No. 453 Squadron would have reached Force Z within an hour. Without fighter cover, the Japanese bombers would have been extremely vulnerable, and it would have been difficult for them to carry out their torpedo attacks. Instead, as the signal was never made, Force Z had to defend itself.

At 1040hrs, the Type 279 radar on *Prince of Wales* detected approaching aircraft. A signal was flashed, warning all of the warships to be in full readiness, and in the flagship Action Stations was sounded, followed by the warning 'Repel Aircraft'. By 1100hrs these aircraft appeared in sight, approaching from the south-west at 3,000m (10,000ft). There were eight of them, all Type 96 bombers from the Mihoro *Kokutai* 1st Squadron. They were in close formation, flying in line abreast, which in theory at least presented the British gunners with an excellent target. As they approached, throughout Force Z the battle ensigns were run up – white ensigns flying from both the foremast and the mainmast on each battleship, with single large ones on the destroyers. The high-angle 4in and 5.25in guns on the two British capital ships tracked their targets. Then the order 'Commence' was given, and the firing began.

At that moment, signal flags appeared on the flagship's foremast. Phillips had ordered the whole force to simultaneously turn 30 deg to starboard. When they first appeared, the enemy planes were just over 16,000 yards away - eight sea miles. By now this had dropped to 11,000m (12,000 yards), and well within range of the high-angle guns. However, the turn threw off the gunners' aims, and they saw the flak bursting well to the right of the

HMS *Prince of Wales* under attack, early afternoon

The British flagship had been crippled by a torpedo hit at 1144hrs that morning. As a result, she was listing heavily to port, her speed reduced to 16 knots and unable to steer a steady course. The list meant that her lower hull on her starboard side was riding high in the water, giving any torpedo hits on that side a good chance of striking her below her protective armoured belt. So, the *Prince of Wales* (1) was extremely vulnerable. Then, at 1220hrs, more Japanese aircraft were spotted, approaching the battleship from the south. Watching their attack develop from the ship's compass platform (2), Admiral Phillips was slow to realise he was under torpedo attack. However, it soon became clear this was exactly what was happening. Due to the list, the battleship's forward 5.25in batteries were unable to depress low enough to fire at the approaching low-flying aircraft. Her after batteries were out of action due to a lack of electrical power. Only the ship's multiple-barrelled 'pom-poms' and smaller guns put up any effective defence. The first six Type 1 bombers of the Kanoya *Kokutai* approached the battleship's starboard side from different heights and angles, and released their torpedoes at short range – around 500m. Three of them struck the *Prince of Wales* forward, amidships and aft, causing extensive flooding and irreparable damage. After these mortal blows, the battleship gradually began to sink.

The main armament of the *Prince of Wales* consisted of ten 14in guns, mounted in two four-gun turrets ('A' and 'Y'), and a single two-gun turret ('B'). While these newly designed guns and turrets had teething problems, most of these had been overcome by late 1941 so, if Force Z had reached the Japanese transports, these powerful guns could have wreaked havoc.

approaching aircraft. Still, the High Angle Control System (HACS) the British used was designed to deal with that, and within seconds new targeting information was being passed to the guns. The 4in guns on the *Repulse* opened up at 10,000m (11,000 yards), but they lacked the sophisticated targeting ability of the flagship's more modern weaponry. Meanwhile, the Japanese pilots did not flinch – they kept on coming, heading straight for the *Prince of Wales*.

Then, just as the guns were beginning to find their mark, Phillips ordered another turn, this time of another 50 deg to port, onto a new heading of 055 deg. This effectively masked the port anti-aircraft guns on both British capital ships, but, as the ships' heads swung round, the starboard guns slowly found themselves able to bear again. However, by then, the Japanese bombers had come within 7,500m – just four miles. These manoeuvres were understandable in the circumstances, but they also effectively prevented the British heavy anti-aircraft guns from laying down an effective volume of accurate fire. Only then, as the bombers were almost on top of them, did Phillips order independent manoeuvring – each captain had the freedom to take whatever evasive action he thought best.

For a few tense moments it seemed that the flagship would be the target. However, the moment passed, and the bombers kept flying on towards *Repulse*. The squadron commander, Lieutenant Shirai, rightly supposed she would be the least well-protected of the two capital ships. Then the bombs began to drop. There was not sufficient time to manoeuvre, so all Captain Tennant of the *Repulse* could do was to hope for the best. Seconds later seven huge columns of water rose on both sides of the battlecruiser. On the flagship, they also saw a plume of smoke appear on *Repulse*'s deck, just beside the aircraft hangar. It looked like only one bomb had hit her. On both British ships the anti-aircraft guns had kept on firing throughout the attack – both the heavy 4in and 5.25in guns, but also the smaller 'pom-poms'. Then, as the Japanese planes continued on towards the north, the orders came to cease fire.

Fortunately for *Repulse*, these Japanese bombers carried two 250kg bombs, rather than a single 500kg one. This, though, was bad enough. The bomb hit plunged through the hangar, and into the deck below it – the Royal Marines' mess deck. It went through the deck of that too, before exploding against the armoured deck below it. Below that deck was a boiler room. A heavier bomb would probably have penetrated the armour to explode inside this space. However, the armour held, and the blast was dissipated. In structural terms the damage was slight, nevertheless it started minor fires in the hangar, which had to be extinguished, and more ominously the blast itself had ruptured steam pipes in the engine spaces, scalding several of the engine room staff. Some of them were badly injured, and it took some time to extricate them, and take them to the Sick Bay. On the whole, however, *Repulse* got off fairly lightly.

The Japanese themselves were not unscathed either. Five of Shirai's bombers had been damaged by British fire, and two of them were so badly hit that they were forced to break off the action and head for Kota Bharu, 160 miles away to the north-west. Each of the eight bombers had only dropped one of its two bombs, which meant that Shirai still had six bombs at his disposal, if he wanted to make a second attack. For the moment, though, he was content to get out of range, and give his squadron a chance to regroup. The British were given a brief reprieve, and the chance to deal with their wounded, and brace themselves for the next attack.

The torpedo strike

The lull didn't last long. Ten minutes after the bombers disappeared to the north, the *Prince of Wales*'s radar detected a large force of aircraft approaching from the south-east, flying in two distinct formations. Their height was estimated at 3,000m (10,000ft). These were the two remaining squadrons of the Genzan *Kokutai* – a total of 17 Type 96 twin-engined bombers. The original plan was to launch simultaneous attacks by high-angle bombers and torpedo planes, but now, with the bombers having expended their ordnance on the *Tenedos*, the opportunity for this kind of coordinated attack had been lost. The 1st Squadron was led by Lieutenant Ishihara, who was accompanied by Lieutenant-Commander Nakanishi. He was the second-in-command of the *Kokutai*, and the senior officer now that Captain Maeda had returned to Saigon with the bombers of the 3rd Squadron. The 2nd Squadron was commanded by Lieutenant Takai, who described his first sighting of the British ships:

> At exactly 1.03pm [1133hrs] a black spot was sighted, directly beneath the cloud ahead of us. It appeared to be the enemy vessels, about 25 miles away… Soon we could distinguish the ships. The fleet was composed of two battleships, escorted by three destroyers and one small merchant vessel. The battleships were the long-awaited *Prince of Wales* and the *Repulse*!

In fact, the merchant ship – the *Haldis* – wasn't part of the British force, it just happened to be nearby, probably too close for her crew. As the 17 bombers drew closer, Lieutenant-Commander Nakanishi ordered them to form up into their attack formation. Essentially, this meant that each squadron formed up with one plane behind the other, forming a long column of eight or nine planes. Then, Nakanishi gave the order to attack.

As Takai recalled:

> The enemy fleet was now about eight miles away. We were still flying at 2,500m and were in the ideal position to attack. As we had planned, Nakanishi's bomber increased its speed and began to drop towards the enemy fleet. He was heading to the right, and a little ahead of the warships. Trying to maintain the same distance and not be left behind, the bombers of my squadron also increased their speed as I started a gradual dive.

In both British capital ships each of these eight-barrelled 2-pounder 'pom-poms' was mounted so as to cover a prescribed arc of fire around the ship. In theory these would combine to give the ship all-round protection. In practice, though, the weapons' weight of fire was insufficient to offer an effective defence.

The Genzan *Kokutai* had trained hard for this moment – and for this kind of attack. According to their pre-arranged deployment, the 1st Squadron would attack the largest vessel – in this case the *Prince of Wales* – while the 2nd Squadron would attack the second-largest warship – the *Repulse*. As the aircraft were approaching the British ships from the south-east, the British ships were both roughly bow-on to the approaching bombers, with the *Repulse* just under a mile to the west of the flagship.

This meant that Takai began leading his squadron over to the left, to attack the battlecruiser, while Ishihara's column of planes headed towards the right, and the battleship. The aim was to launch simultaneous attacks from opposite sides of the British formation. If the bomber squadron had not attacked the *Tenedos*, these two squadrons would go in while the third squadron would simultaneously carry out its attack overhead. They were still out of range of the British anti-aircraft guns, but during this approach they would be especially vulnerable to attack from enemy fighters. However, much to Takai's amazement, there was no sign of any protective air cover, despite being less than 40 minutes' flying time from Singapore.

On board the flagship, Admiral Phillips had been warned that a new wave of aircraft were approaching, having been detected by radar. He ordered the force to increase speed to 25 knots, but he maintained the same south-easterly course. This time he signalled that all ships could manoeuvre independently. He was on the battleship's compass platform, so he had a good view of the approaching threat. When warned by the battleship's torpedo officer that he thought they were planning a torpedo attack, Phillips reportedly disagreed. He still seemed to think he would be attacked by high-flying bombers. As they watched, the Japanese bombers had split into two groups – both long columns of aircraft, with one heading across their bows to the east, and the other opening the angle by heading from left to right, to the west, and the *Repulse*. A patch of low cloud temporarily hid the left-hand group of aircraft, but by then the bombers were being tracked by radar, and by the HACS guiding the battleship's 5.25in guns.

By 1141hrs the nine bombers of Ishihara's squadron reached a point 12,000m (13,000 yards) off the port beam of the battleship. She was heading towards the south-east, and they were roughly flying parallel to it, to the north-east of the British flagship. Their height had also dropped to less than 1,000m (3,280ft). At that moment, Ishihara decided it was time to launch his attack. On his command the three flights of the squadron turned simultaneously to port, until they were heading directly towards the battleship. That meant the squadron was now divided into three groups, each of three aircraft. As they commenced their approach, they dropped down to just under 35m (115ft) – the approved drop height of their Type 91 torpedoes. They were making 150 knots, which compared very favourably with the performance of the obsolete Swordfish torpedo bombers used by Britain's Fleet Air Arm. In fact, several of the watching British sailors thought they were facing a low-level bombing attack, rather than a torpedo attack.

Reputedly, one of those who did not realise the type of threat they faced was Admiral Phillips. When the battleship's torpedo officer told him he thought they were about to face a torpedo attack, the admiral replied that the Japanese did not have any torpedo bombers in the area. If this is true, then he was about to be proved spectacularly wrong. As the approaching planes dropped lower, it became increasingly clear to most that they were carrying out a torpedo run. Obviously, the *Prince of Wales* fired back with everything she could, with the weight of fire coming from the four twin 5.25in turrets on the battleship's port side. They were operating under 'controlled fire', directed by the HACS, and augmented by radar. In other words, fire was controlled centrally.

The 5.25in Quick-Firer Mark I had a rate of fire of seven to eight rounds a minute. The turrets had a relatively slow training rate of 10 deg a second, but as the bombers were heading directly towards the ship this was not a problem. After 12 rounds per gun – roughly 90 seconds of fire – the Japanese had come within 2,750m (3,000 yards) of the battleship – 40 seconds of flying time. At that point, the guns were switched to 'barrage fire', which meant

On the *Prince of Wales*, anti-aircraft gunnery direction was based on the Mark IV HACS system, but augmented by fire control radars, such as these Type 285 sets, which were linked to her 5.25in batteries. This photograph also shows seamen manning binocular direction sets, used as an emergency form of gunnery direction.

Location: 75 nautical miles south-east of Kuantan, Malaya

Scattered cloud cover: 5/10ths at 3,000m

Wind: North-East, 15 knots. Sea State 3. Visibility Good

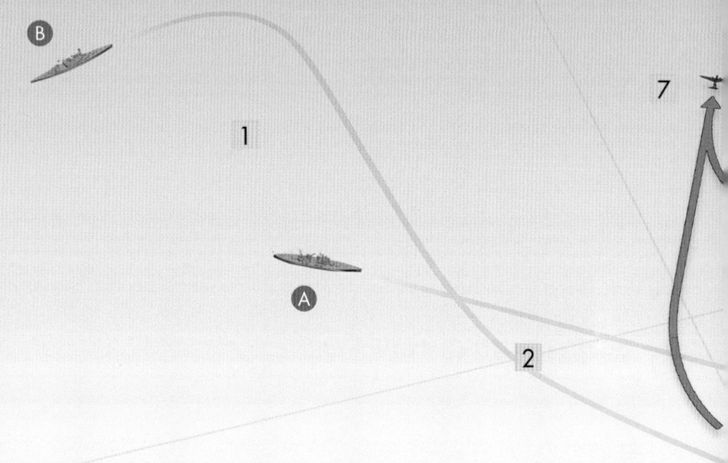

EVENTS

1 1220hrs. Approaching enemy aircraft spotted by radar and lookouts in Force Z

2 1221hrs. Warships of Force Z open fire on the attackers

3 1223hrs. Elements of the 1st and 2nd squadrons, Kanoya *Kokutai* attack *Prince of Wales*. Flagship hit by three torpedoes on her starboard side. These cause extensive flooding, and more loss of propulsive power

4 1224hrs. The remainder of 1st and 2nd squadrons, Kanoya *Kokutai* break away from the attack on the *Prince of Wales*, and begin a run towards the *Repulse*, which is off their port side. They circle around the battlecruiser, to attack her from several directions at once

5 1224hrs. *Repulse* avoids most of these torpedoes. However, one hits *Repulse* on her port quarter, damaging her outer port propeller shaft and causing flooding

6 1225hrs. Simultaneously, the 3rd Squadron, Kanoya *Kokutai* have been approaching the battlecruiser from both port and starboard. *Repulse* struck by four more torpedoes, three on her port side and one to starboard. These cause extensive flooding damage, jam her rudder, and the battlecruiser begins to heel over and sink. The order is given to abandon ship

7 1230hrs. Attack by the Kanoya *Kokutai* ends as the aircraft head for their home bases

8 1232hrs. *Repulse* sinks

9 1240hrs. A fresh wave of Japanese aircraft appears

10 1241hrs. The 1st and 2nd squadrons, Mihoro *Kokutai* conduct a high-level bombing attack on *Prince of Wales*

11 1244hrs. *Prince of Wales* struck amidships by a 500kg bomb, causing extensive casualties

1310hrs. On *Prince of Wales* the order is given to abandon ship

1315hrs. *Prince of Wales* begins to capsize

1323hrs. *Prince of Wales* sinks

The second wave

1220–1323hrs, Wednesday 10 December 1941

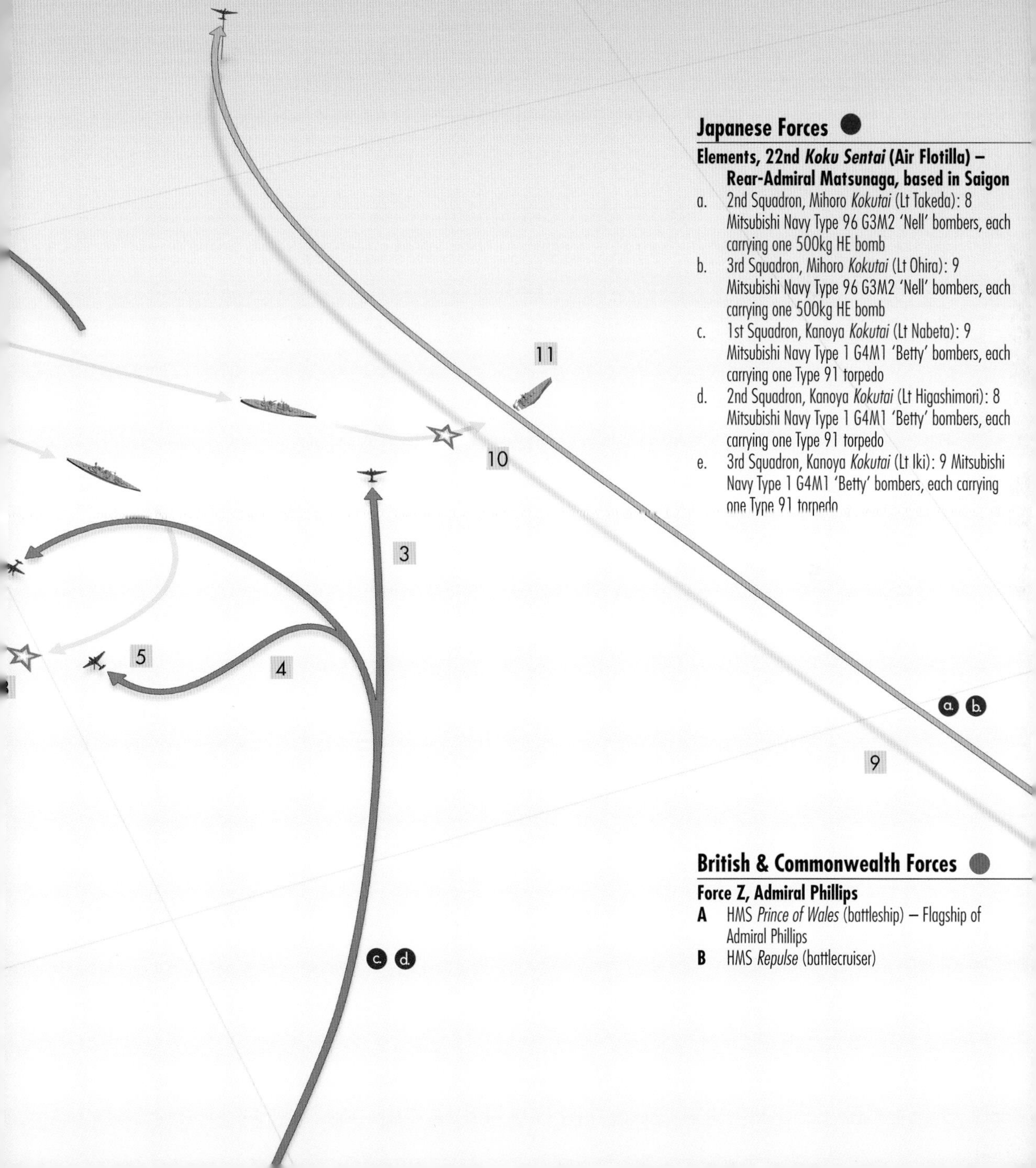

Japanese Forces

Elements, 22nd *Koku Sentai* (Air Flotilla) – Rear-Admiral Matsunaga, based in Saigon

a. 2nd Squadron, Mihoro *Kokutai* (Lt Takeda): 8 Mitsubishi Navy Type 96 G3M2 'Nell' bombers, each carrying one 500kg HE bomb
b. 3rd Squadron, Mihoro *Kokutai* (Lt Ohira): 9 Mitsubishi Navy Type 96 G3M2 'Nell' bombers, each carrying one 500kg HE bomb
c. 1st Squadron, Kanoya *Kokutai* (Lt Nabeta): 9 Mitsubishi Navy Type 1 G4M1 'Betty' bombers, each carrying one Type 91 torpedo
d. 2nd Squadron, Kanoya *Kokutai* (Lt Higashimori): 8 Mitsubishi Navy Type 1 G4M1 'Betty' bombers, each carrying one Type 91 torpedo
e. 3rd Squadron, Kanoya *Kokutai* (Lt Iki): 9 Mitsubishi Navy Type 1 G4M1 'Betty' bombers, each carrying one Type 91 torpedo

British & Commonwealth Forces

Force Z, Admiral Phillips

A HMS *Prince of Wales* (battleship) – Flagship of Admiral Phillips
B HMS *Repulse* (battlecruiser)

On 8 December 1941 the *Repulse* followed the flagship to sea. Here she is seen in the Jahore Strait, just off the Singapore Naval Base, before beginning the passage out to the open sea. She was still sporting her distinctive black and light grey camouflage scheme.

their shells were set to explode in front of the oncoming aircraft, to put them off their aim. By then the closer-range weapons had joined in. The battleship carried a single 40mm Bofors gun, crewed by the Royal Marines, as well as six eight-barrelled 2-pounder 'pom-poms'. The latter was not a particularly great weapon, and only four of them could bear on the attackers. Still, their weight of fire was impressive. During the final moments singly mounted Lewis light machine guns even joined in, although these were of no practical use.

This weight of fire, though, still did not seem to stop the Japanese. They kept on coming, and the planes were now approaching their release point, less than a mile off the battleship's port beam. The inability to stop or break up the attack was partly down to the failure of the battleship's HACS system to deal with a high-speed torpedo attack of this kind. Afterwards, gunners felt the controlled fire of the 5.25in guns was repeatedly off-target. Another problem was the 2-pounder 'pom-poms', which kept jamming. The poor performance might also have been exacerbated by the movement of the ship itself, as she was starting to turn hard to port. Then, the Japanese bombers started dropping their torpedoes. The range varied according to the skill and verve of the air crews, some dropped at the textbook range of 1,500m from the target, while other pilots waited until they had closed to within 600m.

In fact, the British fire was not completely ineffective. One of the bombers, piloted by Petty Officer Kawada, was hit just after it launched its torpedo. It was later claimed he had tried to ram his stricken plane into the battleship, but the British observers reported her simply plunging into the sea. Three other bombers were damaged by anti-aircraft fire, but none of them were prevented from launching their torpedoes, or for that matter making it back to base. By now, though, the torpedoes were on their way. One reportedly broke up when it hit the water, but the other eight landed well and were soon on their way to the target.

The Type 91 Model 1 torpedo had a speed of 42 knots – less than 100mph slower than the bombers carrying them – so, depending on the range from the ship when they were dropped, their run would take anything between 26 and 62 seconds. Therefore, they were not being aimed at the spot the battleship occupied when they were launched. Instead, the crews 'led' the target, aiming at a point they expected her to reach by the time the torpedo reached the same spot. This of course relied on the battleship steering a straight course. However, Captain Leach had no intention of doing this, and at this stage the *Prince of Wales* was turning hard to port, as Leach tried to 'comb' the tracks of the oncoming torpedoes. He almost did it. Most of these torpedoes would speed harmlessly past the hull of the battleship, while another, the most southerly torpedo, would actually pose a threat to the *Repulse*, now a mile away to the south-west. However, try as he might, Leach could not evade them all. Two of these eight torpedoes would hit their mark.

Meanwhile, after releasing their torpedoes, the Japanese pilots continued to point their machines towards the battleship. The trouble was, they couldn't easily bank away without presenting a better target to the British gunners, so their tactic was to fly on and strafe the battleship, before passing over her, then heading away to safety. This is exactly what several of the planes did, and hundreds of 7.7mm (0.3in) bullets struck the battleship's superstructures, causing several casualties before the planes sped overhead. As the planes roared in they were only a few seconds ahead of their torpedoes. On the bridge of *Prince of Wales*, Leach watched anxiously as he observed the bubbling tracks move towards the ship, and while most passed safely, two tracks were leading towards the battleship's port quarter, one slightly ahead of the other.

Captain Aylwin of the Royal Marines was manning a 'pom-pom' mounted on top of 'Y' turret when he saw the first of these two torpedoes strike the port side of the ship below the turret: 'Suddenly there was the most terrific jolt accompanied by a loud explosion immediately where I was standing on the port side. A vast column of water and smoke shot up into the air, to a height of about 200ft, drenching the quarterdeck.' He reported a vast shudder running through the ship. Others likened it to a collision, accompanied by the hull lifting slightly, bouncing and shaking. Then they all felt the intense vibration, which lasted about 30 seconds. The cause could be found beneath the hull, where the propeller shaft entered the ship. The torpedo had struck the battleship's stern immediately forward of the 'A-shaped' propeller bracket serving the battleship's port-side outboard propeller.

Almost simultaneously the second torpedo may have struck the ship amidships, just below the battleship's mainmast. However, it has also been convincingly argued that this exploded prematurely, just before striking the hull. Possibly, this was due to it being caught in the blast of the first torpedo. Certainly, divers inspecting the hull afterwards didn't find any visible damage in the area the torpedo is supposed to have struck. In any case, its blast was largely absorbed by the ship's anti-torpedo bulge, and so it caused little damage, apart from some local flooding in four small watertight compartments. The real damage then, was caused by the first torpedo, which struck the ship at 1144hrs. It buckled the propeller shaft, which was still rotating at high speed and which caused such intense vibration that it was felt throughout the ship. It was clear that something serious had happened, but on the battleship's bridge, the full extent of the damage was not immediately apparent.

The juddering vibration lasted about half a minute. By the end of it the men on the bridge noted that the battleship's speed was dropping, and she was taking on a pronounced list to port. All this time they were still dodging torpedoes – the last of them passed the starboard side of the battleship at 1145hrs. On the compass platform, both Admiral Phillips and Captain Leach said little – they were waiting for damage reports, but clearly the violence of the unexpected torpedo attack had taken them by surprise. One observer described both officers as looking stunned. Of course by then they would both have realised that the battleship had suffered a serious blow. The list to port was now 11.5 deg, and the ship's speed had dropped to just 16 knots. But this attack was not the end of it. The radar operators and lookouts reported another wave of aircraft were approaching, and this time they were headed towards the *Repulse*.

A mile to the west, Captain Tennant of the *Repulse* had seen the attack develop, and hoped that Captain Leach's turn was enough. Then they saw the column of water rise up over the battleship, followed by another. There was nothing they could do – in fact, the attack posed a threat to *Repulse* too. One of the torpedoes was heading towards her, and so at 1144hrs Tennant ordered a turn to starboard, away from the oncoming torpedo. It missed the battlecruiser, but Tennant and his men were still keenly aware that another Japanese squadron was nearby, and it could be seen circling them, half hidden by clouds,

The crew of a British destroyer's 4.7in II gun, similar to the weapons mounted in Force Z's two E-class destroyers. The difference, however, is the example shown here was a twin rather than a single gun mounting. Both, though, had a limited anti-aircraft capability.

some miles to the north-west. These were the seven Type 96 torpedo bombers of Lieutenant Takai's 2nd Squadron.

Takai had been reluctant to launch an attack before he could properly identify his target as an enemy ship. To him, *Repulse* looked too similar to the Japanese battlecruiser *Kongo* to be completely certain. Then, through the clouds, he and his observer worked out it wasn't *Kongo* – the Japanese battlecruiser had four main turrets, and this vessel only had three. It was definitely the *Repulse*. This delay in identifying the target meant that Takai had missed the chance to launch a simultaneous attack with Ishihara's squadron. His attack therefore began 12 minutes later. During these minutes Tennant had turned his battlecruiser around to starboard and was now heading towards the east, a mile to the south-west of the flagship. His intention was to approach her, as by now he'd seen two black balls on her foremast – the signal that she was not operating under control. She must have been badly damaged, but so far no other signal had come from the flagship.

Takai's seven bombers were approaching *Repulse* from the north, but overhead there were other Japanese aircraft – the remaining bombers of Lieutenant Shirai's squadron. Each of his six remaining bombers had a single 250kg bomb left, and Shirai intended to use them. Therefore, as Takai's planes were lining up for their own attack, Shirai carried out his own high-level pass. Captain Tennant saw them, but his main focus was on the threat posed by the approaching torpedo planes. At 1156hrs the six bombers released their bombs from a height of 3,500m (11,480ft). Once again, Tennant jinked the battlecruiser, turning to port then starboard, and managed to weave his way through the bombs, six of which fell within 100m (110 yards) of the ship, drenching the men on the upper deck with their spray, and peppering her sides with bomb splinters. Otherwise, they caused no damage.

By then, Takai's planes were making their torpedo run. Afterwards, the Japanese lieutenant described what happened: 'The *Repulse* had already started evasive action, and was making a hard turn to the right. The target angle was becoming smaller and smaller, as the bow of the vessel swung gradually in my direction, making it difficult for me to release a torpedo'. In fact, the battlecruiser was turning to port, and by now the British gunners had opened fire, with single and triple 4in guns and eight-barrelled 'pom-poms', but without much success. The 'pom-poms' kept jamming, while the obsolete 4in guns lacked the sophisticated fire control found in *Prince of Wales*. Still, as Takai put it, 'The air was filled with white smoke, bursting shells, and the tracers of anti-aircraft guns and machine guns.'

The torpedo bombers were now at their release height of 35m (115ft), and Takai recalls his plane approaching the *Repulse* at 200 knots. He couldn't recall the range he launched at – just his pulling of the torpedo release. The time was 1158hrs. The other bombers, extended out in a straggling line to his right, then followed his lead. Moments later the aircraft were flying past the *Repulse*, which was still turning. Those planes that could strafed the battlecruiser before roaring past her, causing several casualties. On the bridge of *Repulse*, Captain Tennant gave a string of orders, which saw the battlecruiser turning to port, then starboard in an attempt to evade the approaching torpedoes. It worked. The old ship shuddered with each turn, but in the end the torpedoes all sped harmlessly by.

The battlecruiser was now to the north-east of the crippled flagship. Just as they avoided the last of these torpedoes, lookouts spotted another wave of aircraft approaching low from the north, off the battlecruiser's port bow. These were the planes led by Lieutenant Takahashi of the Mihoro *Kokutai* 4th Squadron. They had appeared to the north of Force Z, and as Takai's planes made their final run, Takahashi led his squadron forward, and at 1202hrs the eight aircraft dropped their torpedoes from long range, probably 2,000m (2,190 yards), to avoid getting in the way of the bombers ahead of them. At that range it would have taken these Type 91 torpedoes almost a minute and a half to reach the battlecruiser, which was travelling at over 700m a minute, so the chances of hitting her were slim.

The attack over, the bombers curved away and headed for home. Their torpedoes all missed *Repulse*, which meant that, in all, the battlecruiser had successfully evaded 15 torpedoes and 14 bombs in a little over an hour. Captain Tennant modestly heaped the praise on his bridge staff for 'calmly pointing out torpedo-bombing aircraft, which largely contributed to our good fortune in dodging all these torpedoes'. However, it was clear by now that the *Prince of Wales* itself had not been so fortunate. She was to the south of *Repulse* now, and was clearly listing to port and had settled slightly by the stern. Tennant made the decision to close with her, in case the flagship needed his assistance. With hindsight this easily understandable move proved to be a mistake. It would mean that if another torpedo attack developed, the Japanese could easily switch attacks from one ship to the other.

While all this had been going on, Tennant waited in vain for any kind of instructions from the flagship. During a brief lull, he also had a chance to think about air cover – or more accurately the lack of it. He called the battlecruiser's radio room, and was told, to his horror, that so far no request for air cover had been sent from the flagship. It seemed as if Admiral Phillips was still maintaining radio silence, or more likely had forgotten about it when his battleship was hit and crippled. Clearly the time for radio silence was past, so on his own authority Tennant ordered a signal to be sent to the naval base in Singapore, reporting 'enemy aircraft bombing'. This was received at 1204hrs, and within 20 minutes 11 Brewster Buffalos of No. 453 Squadron were scrambled. Unfortunately for both Phillips and Tennant, they would arrive too late.

The mortal blow

What followed was a short gap in the attacks. It gave the crew of both capital ships the chance to take stock and assess the damage. While *Repulse* escaped with only minor damage, it was fast becoming clear that *Prince of Wales* was badly crippled. When the torpedo struck the outer port propeller shaft just forward of the 'A' bracket, the shaft itself was spinning at high speed, so when the torpedo exploded it buckled the shaft and wrecked the bracket. Although the shaft outside the hull was reduced to tangled scrap, it kept spinning, even though it was badly out of alignment. This caused the fearsome vibration which could be felt throughout the ship, and produced a noise likened to a child scraping a stick along park railings – only much louder. The blast also damaged the seal where the shaft entered the hull, causing water to pour into the port-side outer propeller shaft passage.

This shaft passage led all the way forward to 'B engine room', amidships on the battleship's port side and, after surging 200 feet (61m) forward along the shaft passage, it reached the bulkhead at the end, which separated the passage from the engine room. The shaft passed through watertight glands there, but these could not stop the surge, and seawater began pouring into the engine compartment. The engine room crew had already shut the engine down when the vibrations began, and so after trying and failing to stem the flooding, the engine room was abandoned. The last man got out through the watertight hatch just as the surging water reached it. This flooding, though, was only part of the problem. The explosion also ripped a 4m tear in the battleship's lower hull plates, which caused more flooding in the neighbouring port inboard propeller shaft space.

The *Prince of Wales* listing heavily to port, seen from the bridge of the destroyer *Express*. Beneath S3, one of the battleship's after starboard side 5.25in turrets, men can be seen making their way over to the destroyer using ropes and makeshift gangways.

As a result, water began pouring into the ship in several places, and the flooding began working its way forward compartment by compartment. However, the jolt the explosion caused may well have added to the damage caused to the ship's vital generators, which supplied her with electrical power. The battleship had four engine rooms, each associated with its own propeller shaft and boiler room. Each engine also provided steam power to an adjacent Action Machinery Room, where dynamos produced the electricity needed to power the ship's gun turrets and other electrical systems. In addition, there were two diesel dynamo rooms (labelled port and starboard), used as additional sources of electrical power. The initial flooding quickly spread into one of these two dynamo rooms, on the port side of the ship. It also flooded the 'Y Action Machinery Room'. Within a few minutes, two of these dynamo rooms had been flooded, and the dynamos put out of action. That meant that the battleship immediately lost both propulsive power and electrical power.

As in any warship, a long-established damage control system was in place, and well-trained damage control parties were on hand to deal with problems of this kind.

Survivors from the *Repulse* pictured after the sinking of their ship. They were rescued by the destroyers *Electra* and *Vampire*. These men are pictured on board the *Electra*. Their rescue was still under way when *Prince of Wales* was attacked for the last time.

On *Prince of Wales*, however, these men faced a daunting series of challenges. By now the battleship's speed had dropped from 25 knots down to 16 knots, thanks to the loss of the outboard port engine. The flooding had also caused the ship to list to port by as much as 11.5 deg. The flooding was spreading fast, and so unless the damage control parties could stem the flow then the situation would rapidly become much worse. Later, it was estimated that, thanks to this torpedo hit, as much as 2,400 tons of water had entered the ship.

The flooding soon spread to other adjacent compartments. Many of these were vital to the operation of the ship. So far, the three other engine rooms were still fully operational, but then the flooding seeped into 'Y Boiler Room', which until it could be contained meant a drop in steam pressure to 'Y engine', driving the inboard port-side propeller. Just as seriously, the resulting demands on the system meant that two of the remaining dynamos failed, through a combination of a lack of cooling water for the starboard diesel dynamo and the overloading of the dynamo in 'X Action Machinery Room'. Therefore, the remaining dynamos were struggling to provide electrical power to the ship.

The damage control parties did what they could, but they soon found that the loss of electrical power had severed all telephone links in the after part of the ship. That meant the parties had to rely on human runners to pass on reports and request help or equipment. Worse, the after pumps had been put out of action by the flooding. Another problem reported in the subsequent enquiry was that when the torpedoes struck, not all of the ship's watertight doors had been shut, as that morning the tropical heat had rendered many of the machinery spaces unbearably hot. In the subsequent enquiry held in Singapore, the damage control teams were criticised for not correctly prioritising the tasks facing them. While it was important to stem any further flooding, the loss of electrical power was also rapidly compromising the ship's ability to fight back against the enemy.

This loss of power meant that the after 5.25in turrets were also put out of action. That left the *Prince of Wales* with just her forward secondary turrets, but even here the list to port

HMS *Prince of Wales*

Bomb Strike

Torpedo Strike

11.44 am

12.44 pm

12.23 pm

12.24 pm

12.23 pm

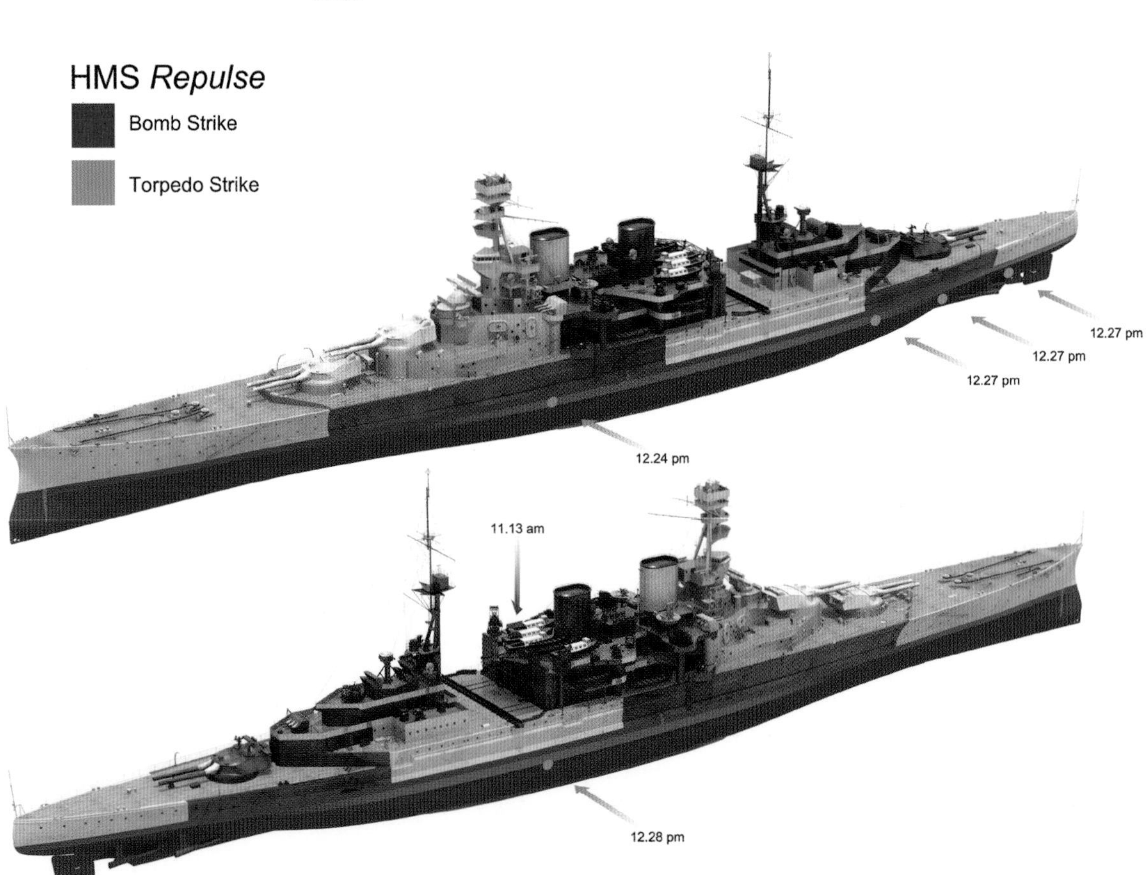

OPPOSITE HITS TO *PRINCE OF WALES* AND *REPULSE*

The first air attack on Force Z began at 1108hrs, when 1st Squadron, Mihoro *Kokutai* conducted a high-level bombing attack on *Repulse.* At 1113hrs, eight 250kg bombs were dropped and one of them struck the battlecruiser on her catapult deck, and penetrated the hangar before exploding. No serious damage was done.

There was a lull of almost half an hour before the next wave of bombers appeared. This time their target was *Prince of Wales.* At 1140hrs, 1st Squadron, Genzan *Kokutai,* launched a torpedo attack on the port side of the British flagship. At 1144hrs, a torpedo struck her outer port-side propeller shaft, damaging it and causing flooding up the shaft tunnel and into the engine room. As a result the battleship's speed was reduced to 16 knots, and she took on a list of 11 deg to port.

There was then a lull in the attacks, until 1220hrs, when the Kanoya *Kokutai* launched a series of attacks on both ships. At 1223hrs *Prince of Wales* was struck by two torpedoes on her starboard side, which damaged her outer starboard propeller shaft and caused flooding forward of the bridge. As a result, the British battleship began to sink. A final hit by a 500kg bomb during a final attack by 3rd Squadron, Mihoro *Kokutai* caused heavy casualties, but did little to hasten the battleship's end. She finally sank at 1323hrs.

Repulse had managed to avoid all of the torpedoes launched at her, but at 1224hrs her luck ran out. She was already manoeuvring to avoid a torpedo attack to starboard, when three torpedo bombers broke away from the attack on *Prince of Wales* and launched their torpedoes at *Repulse* instead. At 1224hrs one struck her amidships on her port side. While this caused some flooding, little major damage was caused.

However, four minutes later another short-range torpedo attack by elements of the Kanoya *Kokutai* resulted in three hits on her port quarter. These caused extensive flooding and damaged her port side propeller shafts. A minute later another torpedo struck amidships on her starboard side, causing heavy flooding. These five torpedo hits in less than five minutes were enough to finish the battlecruiser. She heeled over and sank at 1232hrs.

had rendered the remaining port-side pair of little use, as it was almost impossible to track any approaching targets. Therefore, that one torpedo hit aft had crippled the battleship, and left her air defences unable to cope with the torpedo attacks which were about to follow. The situation *Prince of Wales* found herself in was likened to the loss of the fleet aircraft carrier *Ark Royal* in the Mediterranean less than a month earlier. She had sunk after a single torpedo hit, when flooding led to a loss of power to her engines and dynamos, which in turn stopped her pumps from working.

In *Prince of Wales*, the damage control teams were battling several major crises at the same time, in increasingly difficult conditions, and while still under attack. The loss of the use of her electrical pumps was just as threatening as the loss of her electrically powered steering systems, which made the battleship extremely difficult to steer. Equally threatening was the loss of anti-aircraft capability as the ship was still under air attack. The situation has also been compared with the one the German battleship *Bismarck* found herself in the previous May, but on that occasion, only her steering and some propulsive power had been lost – her weaponry was still fully operational. By comparison, thanks to that single torpedo, the *Prince of Wales* had become little more than a floating target.

As well as the flooding and the damage to her propulsive and electrical systems, the flagship had also lost the use of her air search radar, so had to rely instead on radar warning from *Repulse* and the destroyer escorts, and from her own lookouts. With her steering gear out of action, and only her two starboard engines still working, she had to use her rudder to steer, but that too had lost power, albeit stuck at an angle which helped compensate for the lack of balance to her engines. Captain Leach was therefore unable to steer a straight course, and the battleship continued to veer slightly to port. With the ship barely manoeuvrable, his best defensive option was to try to compensate for the list to port. That way his remaining port-side secondary batteries might still be able to function. Leach therefore ordered the flooding of a series of empty spaces on the battleship's starboard side the ones inside her anti-torpedo bulge.

The initial high-level bombing attack on *Repulse*, taken from one of Lieutenant Shirai's bombers. Bombs land around *Repulse*, and the black smoke amidships denotes the hit scored on the hangar by a 250kg bomb. *Prince of Wales* can be seen in the top of the photograph.

The idea was to compensate for the list, and so bring the ship onto something akin to an even keel. The trouble, though, was that this counter-flooding degraded the battleship's anti-torpedo defences along her starboard side. If another torpedo struck her in this area, then the spaces that should have been voids, designed to absorb the explosion, were now filled with water which would amplify the pressure of the blast, rather than contain it. However, by 1210hrs the counter-flooding had reduced the list to 9 deg, which gave the port-side 5.35in guns a limited ability to train and fire, but this was itself countered by the loss of electrical power to the after secondary guns, and to the communication links between all eight turrets. Still, some progress was being made. Emergency lighting had now been rigged in some key spaces and, having stemmed the flooding, the damage control teams were now working on restoring electrical power to the steering system.

The Japanese Type 93 61cm (24in) torpedo was a devastatingly effective weapon – considerably more so than the Type 91 45cm (17.7in) aerial version used against Force Z. The effectiveness of both torpedoes, though, would come as an unpleasant surprise to the Allies during the opening months of the war. This captured 'Long Lance' is pictured in Washington Navy Yard.

All Captain Leach and his crew needed was time. That, however, was in short supply. Already, lookouts reported seeing more aircraft approaching from the east. At that moment, at around 1215hrs, *Repulse* was roughly a mile to the west of *Prince of Wales*, while the destroyers *Electra* and *Vampire* were astern of the flagship, following Admiral Phillips' order to sweep the area for any men blown overboard by the explosion. *Express* was a mile off the battleship's port beam, her sonar (ASDIC) probing the water for submarines. The destroyer therefore was all that lay between the flagship and the next wave of Japanese aircraft. On board the *Prince of Wales*, the gun crews braced themselves for the attack, having spent the last few minutes stockpiling ammunition by hand, in readiness for the next assault.

The final blow

At 1210hrs, the *Repulse*'s radar room reported that her Type 273 radar had detected multiple aircraft approaching from the south-east. The news was flashed to the *Prince of Wales*, which was still limping along at 16 knots, and veering slightly to port. *Repulse*, though, was making 25 knots, and her crew were now well versed in high-speed manoeuvring and dodging torpedoes. The approaching aircraft were from the Kanoya *Kokutai* – 26 Type 1 torpedo bombers in three squadrons. The formation was led by Lieutenant-Commander Miyauchi, who flew in one of the aircraft of the 1st Squadron. They had actually been on their way back to Dau Mot airfield when the first sighting report of Force Z was made. Miyauchi ordered an immediate change of course. In fact, they had spotted a solitary aircraft first – *Repulse*'s Walrus float plane, flying her anti-submarine patrol. Miyauchi headed towards her, and then, at 1220hrs, they spotted Force Z.

His planes were already low on fuel, so Miyauchi ordered an immediate attack, splitting his aircraft into two groups. The bulk of them – the nine bombers of Lieutenant Nabeta's 1st Squadron and eight from Lieutenant Higashimori's 2nd Squadron – were to attack the largest target, in this case the *Prince of Wales*. That left Lieutenant Iki's nine aircraft of the 3rd Squadron to attack the *Repulse*. The first two squadrons quickly dived down to reach their torpedo release height, and began their runs. On board the *Prince of Wales* there was little Captain Leach could do, apart from try vainly to increase speed, and open up with the few guns which could still fire. As the Japanese were approaching from the battleship's port beam, her ability to fire at her attackers was very limited. As a result, fire from the secondary guns and the 'pom-poms' was completely ineffective.

The *Prince of Wales* was on a south-easterly course, which meant the attackers were off her port bow. However, they then veered round towards the south, and worked their way around so they could approach their target from her starboard side, which, due to the ship's list to port, was exposing her starboard hull below the waterline. The first six bombers approached her off her starboard bow, and the pilots were delighted to find that due to the list, her secondary guns could not depress low enough to shoot them down. To confuse the British, the aircraft approached at slightly different heights and angles. Six Type 91 torpedoes were launched at a range of around 500m (550 yards) – virtually point blank for a torpedo attack, given the need for the warheads to arm. Then the planes flew over the top of the battleship, and were gone. The British could see the approaching torpedo tracks, but could do nothing to avoid them.

With the battleship unable to evade, it was something of a miracle that only three of them struck her. They detonated within seconds of each other, with the first striking the ship forward, just on the starboard side of the bow, followed by another beneath 'B' turret, a little forward of the bridge. Roughly two seconds later the third torpedo hit the battleship's stern, just above the starboard outboard torpedo shaft. The first hit blew a hole right through the bows of the ship, and exited through the battleship's port side. The second was much more deadly, sending a huge column of water towering over the ship, reaching as high as the foremast. Oil also began leaking immediately, presumably from a ruptured fuel tank. The second of these hits also ripped a 20 foot-long (6m) gash in the poorly protected underside of the hull, which caused extensive flooding in the ship's lower decks.

The third torpedo hit struck beneath the quarterdeck, and like the earlier torpedo it buckled the outboard propeller shaft, this time on the ship's starboard side. Again, it caused extensive flooding aft, and again this surged forward along the propeller shaft passage, and into 'A Engine Room'. Essentially, this was a repeat of the very first torpedo hit, which flooded 'B Engine Room'. The engine was quickly shut down, leaving the battleship limping along on just one working engine. It also knocked out more generators, leaving just two still working in the entire ship.

By this stage several thousand tons of water had flooded into the ship. The only advantage of all this was that the additional flooding of starboard compartments had effectively corrected the ship's list to port, but by now she was barely moving, and her upper deck was just a few feet above the sea. Now, the *Prince of Wales* could only make eight knots, and was wallowing along, surrounded by an oil slick. These last blows had caused so much flooding that the damage control parties could not cope with it. Essentially, the ship had reached the point where the flooding couldn't be contained. With every passing minute she settled deeper by the stern.

At that point, Admiral Phillips finally gave permission to break radio silence. He permitted Captain Leach to send a short signal, which said, 'Emergency. Have been struck by a torpedo on the port side. Four torpedoes. *Repulse* hit by one torpedo. Send destroyers.' This was somewhat premature – at that point *Repulse* had only been hit by a small bomb, not a torpedo. Also, by the time the signal was transmitted at 1220hrs, the battleship had been hit three more times. Strangely, still no request was made for air cover, but by now it was far too late for any outside help. Force Z was suffering the consequences of its commander's lack of respect for naval air power.

While this last torpedo attack on the flagship had taken place, *Repulse* had been about a mile to the west, off the battleship's starboard quarter, so Captain Tennant and his bridge crew were able to see the three torpedo hits quite clearly. They had no time to watch for more than a second, though, because yet more aircraft were spotted off their starboard beam,

Boats are launched from the destroyer *Electra* to go out in search of more crewmen from *Repulse*. The destroyer's decks are already crammed with survivors from the battlecruiser. The rescue attempt continued well into the afternoon.

and turning to carry out an attack from different directions. At 1220hrs, eight bombers drawn from the first two squadrons of the Kanoya *Kokutai* dropped their torpedoes at long range – around 1,500m (1,640 yards) – and Tennant had just enough time to swing his ship round to starboard, to successfully comb the torpedo tracks. However, this involved committing the old battlecruiser to a hard turn at speed, and just over a mile to the east, two squadrons of torpedo bombers were already lined up for their attack on the flagship.

Off the battlecruiser's port quarter, they could see these other torpedo planes carrying out their attack run on the *Prince of Wales*, and banking to the left. On Nabeta's orders they were targeting the battlecruiser's port side. They launched from long range – almost 2,000m (2,190 yards), which meant the run would take about 80 seconds. The *Repulse* was already committed to her turn to comb the eight torpedoes already in the water to the west, so this time there was nothing Captain Tennant could do. He had finally been caught out. At 1221hrs a torpedo struck the battlecruiser amidships on her port side, and blew a hole in her outer hull, but this was where her anti-torpedo bulge was at its thickest, and the blast was dissipated without causing any serious damage, apart from some minor flooding.

Repulse started listing slightly as her outer void compartments flooded, but the prompt counter-flooding of some starboard watertight compartments kept the battlecruiser on a reasonably even keel. Another torpedo bumped along the side of the ship, without exploding due to the angle. The third torpedo missed completely. So far, Tennant had been reasonably successful at dodging the oncoming torpedoes. Out of 16 launched at him, only one had struck the battlecruiser, and it hadn't caused any major damage. This run of good fortune, though, was about to come to an end. The 3rd Kanoya Squadron was still circling around the two British capital ships, while Lieutenant Iki waited for the right moment. He now ordered

As the *Prince of Wales* continued to list further to port, Captain Leach gave the order to abandon ship. Here, men can be seen sliding down ropes onto the deck of the destroyer *Express*, or lowering themselves over the side of the battleship. Moments before, the makeshift gangways spanning the gap had fallen into the sea as the gap between the ships widened.

his nine aircraft to split up, and attack the battlecruiser from both sides. Two flights – six aircraft in total – worked their way around to the north, then turned to approach the *Repulse* from her starboard beam. Meanwhile, the last flight of three aircraft did the same from the south, towards the battlecruiser's port side.

The three bombers approaching her port side came within 500m (550 yards) before launching their torpedoes. The aircraft then strafed the *Repulse* as they flew over her. But the *Repulse*'s gunners fought back. Lieutenant Iki's plane was damaged as it passed over the battlecruiser, while a second, hit by 2-pounder shells, exploded in a fireball. The third was also hit by point-blank fire from a turret-mounted 'pom-pom', and crashed into the sea to the west of the ship. Petty Officers Taue and Momoi and their crews were all killed, but just moments later they had their revenge. All three torpedoes struck the port side of *Repulse*, one amidships, the second below 'X' turret and the third right at the stern. That last torpedo, probably launched from Iki's plane, jammed the battlecruiser's rudder, forcing her to steam in a wide, lazy circle to starboard. This, though, was only the start of it.

While this attack was going in, the six remaining aircraft of the squadron approached *Repulse* from the north, heading towards her starboard beam. These bombers released their torpedoes at a longer range – around 1,200m (1,310 yards), which gave them a running time of about 50 seconds. At 1225hrs, one of them struck the battlecruiser's starboard side, just level with 'E Boiler Room', which caused extensive flooding. The other torpedoes missed their target, but it was clear that *Repulse*'s luck had run out. In the space of four minutes she had been struck by five torpedoes – four on her port side, and one to starboard. The ship was flooding in several places, and was now listing 12 deg to port. Her electrical systems had begun to fail, and internal communications were not working. She also had a jammed rudder. Captain Tennant was forced to bow to the inevitable, and gave the order, 'Cease all work in the ship below', that would bring the men topside, ready for the order to abandon ship.

By 1230hrs the last of these torpedo planes had flown out of range. They were already heading off towards the north, in the direction of their home airfields in Indochina. All of the torpedo-carrying bombers had carried out their attacks. All that was left to the Japanese were the two remaining squadrons of high-level bombers from the Mihoro *Kokutai* but by now it was clear that *Prince of Wales* was badly crippled, while *Repulse* was sinking. On the battlecruiser, Captain Tennant ordered the Carley floats to be cut loose, and gathered whatever men he could on the battlecruiser's upper decks. It was all done in a very orderly way – there was no sign of panic, or of men disobeying orders. Tennant ordered the destroyers *Electra* and *Vampire* to stand by, ready to pick up the men in the water. Then he gave the order to abandon ship.

The tragedy was, thanks to the breakdown in internal communications, these orders never reached many of the compartments in the bowels of the ship. Some men realised what was happening, and when the ship's list became increasingly severe they made their way to the upper deck as best they could. Others left it too late, and found themselves trapped. As Tennant put it later:

> When the ship had a list of 30° to port I looked over the side and saw the Commander and two or three hundred men collecting on the starboard side. I never saw the slightest sign of panic or ill-discipline. I told them how well they had fought, and wished them good luck as they jumped into the oil-fouled sea. The ship hung on for several minutes with a list of 60 or 70° to port, and then rolled over.

At that point the cries of men trapped inside could still be heard through ventilation ducts. Most of the crew slithered down the starboard side of the hull and into the sea. Again, there was no sign of panic. Captain Tennant was one of the last of them, swept into the sea as his ship went under. The battlecruiser rolled over on her beam ends, with her masts lying parallel to the water. She paused for a minute or so, then continued to roll over. Her stern came out of the water, before slipping under again, and dragging the rest of the ship with her. For a few moments her bow rose above the surface, and then it too disappeared. The time was now 1232hrs. All that was left of her was an oil slick, debris and hundreds of oil-covered men. The two destroyers closed in to pick up whomever they could. Over to the west, the crew of the *Prince of Wales* saw their consort go down, but there was nothing they could do to help as they were too busy trying to keep their own ship from following her to the bottom.

Just nine minutes later, at 1241hrs, lookouts on the flagship spotted another squadron of aircraft approaching – high-level bombers, approaching from the east at 2,560m (8,400ft). Lieutenant Takeda's squadron was flying in a very tight formation, with all eight Type 96 bombers heading, and made their approach almost directly towards the battleship's bows. The *Prince of Wales* fired back as best she could. This time her forward 5.25in guns fired, together with the 'pom-poms' and other light guns, but it did no good. On the compass platform Captain Leach watched the bombs fall, and warned everyone to hit the deck. Seven 500kg bombs were dropped – one bomber failed to release its payload – and one of them hit its target. The bomb landed on the port side of the catapult deck, then plunged on to explode against the armoured deck below. In between was the cinema flat, used as an emergency first-aid station. It was crowded with men – up to 300 of them, and the blast ripped through the crowd, maiming and killing many of the already injured men.

Structurally, with one important exception, the bomb hit did not do much damage. In terms of the battleship's crew and their morale though, its effect was devastating. The blast and flash also filtered through to other neighbouring compartments and even down into 'X Boiler room', causing more casualties, and cutting the steam power to 'X Engine Room'. That effectively put the battleship's last remaining engine out of business, and the *Prince of Wales* slid to a halt, wallowing in the waves while inside her hull the flooding kept on spreading. It was clear now that the battleship was sinking, and the fight to save her was all but hopeless. Captain Leach, however, refused to bow to the inevitable. He sent another message to Singapore, requesting tugs to tow the flagship home, but by now she'd taken on nearly 18,000 tons of water, and nothing but a miracle could save her.

At that point, Leach ordered the destroyer *Express* to come alongside, to help take off the wounded. Others were lowered onto Carley floats, and set adrift, where they could be picked up by the three destroyers. The guns had stopped firing, as by now the last of the Japanese bombers had flown out of range. Some of the survivors remember how quiet it all seemed. Those who could had gathered on the upper deck, and were readying themselves for the order to abandon ship. Instead, Leach came down from the bridge and moved among them, asking for volunteers to help him nurse the ship back to Singapore. Many of the men stepped forward. Leach then ordered the remainder, apart from the gunners manning the anti-aircraft defences, to make their way over to the *Express*. However, it soon became clear that the situation was hopeless. Instead, Leach ordered the crew to inflate their lifejackets.

With that, Captain Leach returned to the bridge, where Admiral Phillips was waiting calmly for the end. At 1300hrs, Leach ordered the remaining engine room staff to save themselves.

That, then, just left the men manning the ship's remaining air defences. Meanwhile, gangplanks were rigged between the battleship and the destroyer, and men began crossing over them. Lines were thrown, and more men began sliding down them to safety, until willing hands pulled them safely aboard the *Express*. Then, at 1315hrs, the *Prince of Wales* lurched a little more to port, and the gap between the two warships widened. The gangplanks fell into the gap between the two ships. Men still slid down the ropes, but one by one these parted, and several men fell into the sea. Others tried to jump from one ship to the other, but few made it.

The lurch almost capsized the *Express*. The battleship's starboard anti-torpedo bulge rose out of the water, and for a moment it threatened to flip the destroyer on her beam end. Lieutenant-Commander Cartwright managed to work her free, and she pulled away a few yards, but the bump had left a 7m-long (23 ft) gash in the destroyer's port side, just above the waterline. Meanwhile, Cartwright's crew lowered nets and ropes, and began hauling men aboard. That was the point that Leach finally gave the order to abandon ship. Gratefully, the gunners left their posts, and joined the throng of men on the starboard side of the upper deck, sliding down the sloping hull into the oil-covered water. Soon the side of the ship and the water off her port side were covered in men. Many injured themselves, or were killed, but the majority made it, and began swimming away to safety. The fear now was that the ship would sink, and pull them down with it.

The *Prince of Wales* slowly heeled over onto her port side. She hung there, almost on her beam ends for a few minutes, and groups of men were seen still walking around on her hull, while others were seen sitting on it, resigned to their fate and waiting for the end. Inside the ship, hundreds of others had either not heard the order to abandon ship, or had left it too late, and were now trapped. The stern sank first, but compared to the *Repulse* the flagship sank slowly, even reluctantly. Most of the men left on the battleship's upper deck were now concentrated on the forecastle – now the highest part of the ship. Again, there was little or no sense of panic. On board the *Express* or from a safe distance away in the water, hundreds of men watched as the battleship slowly began to slip under. Her bow rose in the air, revealing the hole caused by a Japanese torpedo. More men jumped, and then she slipped under the surface, pulling many down with her. By 1323hrs she had gone.

Now, all that remained of Force Z were its three destroyers, busily hauling oil-covered survivors from the sea. Ironically, three minutes earlier the roar of approaching aircraft had been heard. The last squadron of Japanese bombers had remained circling the area to the north, waiting to see if their bombs were still needed. However, it wasn't them. These newcomers were Brewster Buffalos – four fighters from No. 453 Squadron. Another seven would arrive a little later. The Japanese bombers darted away into the clouds to the north, but the fighters didn't give chase. Instead, they had appeared at 1320hrs, just as the upturned *Prince of Wales* began to sink from view, and an hour too late to make a difference. Flight Lieutenant Vigors, commanding the flight, claimed seeing men waving and cheering him as he swept past. He saw it as an uplifting patriotic gesture. The truth, however, was a little different. According to survivors, the men in the water were booing the airmen, for arriving too late to save them.

These were the planes summoned by Captain Tennant of the *Repulse*. Throughout the action, just as he had all the way through the operation, Admiral Phillips never sought air cover for his ships. Now he paid the price. When the *Prince of Wales* sank, 327 officers and men of her crew went down with her. The casualties included both Admiral Phillips and Captain Leach, both of whom were drowned when the battleship sank beneath them. However, 1,285 of their battleship's crew were rescued, mostly by *Express*, whose decks were crowded with men. Four miles to the east, 513 men were lost when *Repulse* sank, from a total crew of 1,309. Captain Tennant was one of the lucky ones. Japanese casualties, by contrast, were just 18 men – the crew of three bombers. The final death toll was 840 men from the two capital ships. It was a high price to pay for such a salutary lesson in the dominance of naval airpower, and the obsolescence of the battleship.

ANALYSIS

The news of the loss of *Prince of Wales* and *Repulse* reached Singapore before their escorting destroyers had finished picking up survivors. At 1318hrs, as the capsized battleship was in her final moments, the destroyer *Electra* signalled Singapore with the news, 'HMS *Prince of Wales* sunk'. Other signals would follow, giving more details, including the fact that *Repulse* had also been lost. The task of informing the Admiralty fell to Rear-Admiral Palliser, then in Singapore Naval Base. At 1345hrs he signalled the Admiralty, reporting that both capital ships had been sunk by torpedoes. According to Lieutenant Dyer of *Tenedos*, who reported to him that evening, the admiral was still severely shaken by the news. Any notion of covering up the scale of the disaster was foolhardy – the Japanese Navy were quick to claim full credit for the victory in a radio broadcast transmitted at 1435hrs.

The *Prince of Wales*, pictured in the Pentland Firth off Orkney in early May 1941, shortly before accompanying the battlecruiser *Hood* in her hunt for the German battleship *Bismarck*. In the battle of the Denmark Strait which followed, the *Prince of Wales* was hit eight times, and forced to break off the action.

It provided full, but not completely accurate, details of the attack, and reported the loss of both British ships off Kuantan in an attack begun at 1215hrs that day. Therefore, Palliser, in conjunction with Brooke-Popham, notified the local press and radio stations. Soon the news from both sources was picked up elsewhere, and transmitted around the world. In London, Prime Minister Churchill was woken up with the news that *Prince of Wales* and *Repulse* had been lost, and that Admiral Phillips had drowned. He later described it as the most grievous blow he suffered during the entire course of the war. At 1132hrs (1832hrs in Singapore time), Churchill broke the news to the House of Commons. In his announcement, he quoted the Japanese communiqué that stated both ships had been sunk by air attack. The survivors of Force Z were still on their way home at this point. They arrived back in Singapore Naval Base at 2310hrs that evening. Meanwhile, in Saigon, the young Japanese air crews were busy celebrating a glorious victory.

It certainly was an incredible achievement – a real turning point in naval history. The Royal Navy had lost two powerful capital ships, and its whole strategic position in the Far East had unravelled over the course of just two hours. Since the battle of Jutland in 1916, the navy hadn't lost two capital ships in a single action. For those like Admiral Phillips, who viewed the battleship as the dominant force in naval warfare, this was a real body blow. Until now,

no capital ship had been sunk at sea by enemy aircraft. While the loss of *Repulse* was extremely unfortunate, it could be argued that she was an old ship, and a battlecruiser, so she lacked the weaponry and protection of more modern capital ships. The same excuse, however, could not be used to mitigate the loss of the *Prince of Wales.* She was less than a year old, and was one of only three such modern battleships in service. Neither ship was able to defend herself against a heavy and determined air attack, carried out by well-trained airmen.

As battles go, the sinking of Force Z was an amazingly one-side affair. The anti-aircraft weaponry provided to these two capital ships had proved unequal to the task. The much-vaunted HACS system had failed to direct sufficient fire at the attackers to deter either high-level bombers or low-level attacks by torpedo-carrying planes. While the lighter anti-aircraft weapons had proved more effective, the 2-pounder 'pom-pom' barrels had jammed repeatedly, and the smaller 40mm Bofors and 20mm Oerlikon mounts had lacked the fire control systems which could render their fire more effective. While the air warning radar fitted to *Prince of Wales* had detected the approaching aircraft, and the Type 285 system had worked well in targeting the approaching aircraft on behalf of the

	HMS *Repulse* – Renown class battlecruiser	HMS *Prince of Wales* – King George V-class battleship
Laid Down:	January 1915 (John Brown, Clydebank)	January 1937 (Cammell Laird, Birkenhead, Merseyside)
Launched:	January 1916. Completed: August 1916	May 1939. Completed: January 1941
Displacement:	32,740 tons (fully laden)	43,786 tons (fully laden)
Length (overall):	794ft 3in (242.1m)	745ft 1in (227.1m)
Beam:	90ft (27.4m)	103ft 2in (31.4m)
Draught:	29ft 8in (9m)	34ft 4in (10.5m)
Propulsion:	4x Brown-Curtis geared turbines, 8x Babcock & Wilcox boilers, 4x propellers, generating 112,000shp	4x Parsons geared turbines, 8x Admiralty boilers, 4x propellers, generating 110,000shp
Maximum Speed:	30.5 knots	28.3 knots
Range:	3,650 nautical miles at 10 knots	15,600 nautical miles at 10 knots
Armament:	6x 15in (38.1cm) BL Mark I guns, in three twin turrets 9x 4in (10.2cm) Mark IX QF guns in three triple mounts 6x 4in (10.2cm) Mark V QF guns in single mounts 16x 2-pounder 'pom-pom' Mark VIII AA guns in two eight-barrelled mounts 16 x 0.5in machine guns, in four quadruple mounts 8x 20mm Oerlikon AA guns in single mounts 8x 21in torpedo tubes, in two quadruple mounts	10x 14in BL Mark VII guns, in one twin and two quadruple turrets 16x 5.25in dual-purpose QF Mark I guns in eight twin turrets 48x 2-pounder 'pom-pom' Mark VIII AA guns in six eight-barrelled mounts 1x 40mm Bofors AA gun in single mount 7x 20mm Oerlikon AA guns in single mounts
Armour:	Belt: 2–9in (5.1–22.9cm) Deck: 1–4in (2.5–10.2cm) Turret Faces: 11in (28cm) Turret Sides and Barbettes: 4–7in (10.2–17.8cm) Bulkheads: 3–4in (7.6–10.2cm) Conning Tower: 10in (25.4cm)	Belt: 4.5–14.7in (11.4–37cm) Deck: 5–6in (12.7–15.2cm) Turrets and Barbettes: 12.75in (32.4cm) Bulkheads: 10–12in (25.4–30.5cm) Conning Tower: 3–4in (7.6–10.2cm)
Sensors:	Type 273 surface search radar, Types 284 and 286 fire control radars	Type 279 air search radar, Type 271 surface search radar, Types 282, 284 and 285 fire control radars
Aircraft:	4x Supermarine Walrus float planes, with one catapult	4x Supermarine Walrus float planes, with one catapult
Complement:	1,309 officers and men	1,612 officers and men

battleship's secondary batteries, they failed to actually throw up a sufficiently heavy weight of fire to stop the attack.

Of the 16 Japanese bombers which conducted high-level bombing attacks on Force Z, none of the aircraft had been shot down, even though they were exactly the type of target the HACS system had been designed to deal with. However, ten of the bombers had been damaged during their bombing runs. This, then, suggests that the fault did not lie with the gunnery direction – it was more a problem caused by the lack of effectiveness of the 4in and 5.25in guns which fired at the Japanese planes. Incidentally, these 16 Japanese aircraft scored two hits on Force Z – one on each capital ship. The statistics emerging from the torpedo attacks were even more revealing. Here, 50 Japanese bombers carried out low-level torpedo attacks, and, of these, 17 were damaged. Three more bombers were shot down. Here, the British heavy anti-aircraft guns were singularly ineffective. Instead, most of the damage and all of the kills were almost certainly achieved by Force Z's lighter anti-aircraft guns.

The lesson British and American analysts took from this was that these larger anti-aircraft guns were not particularly effective against torpedo bombers. Their performance would improve of course, later in the war, with the development of better and more integrated fire control systems, incorporating better versions of HACS, efficient air search

OPPOSITE
One of the unsung heroes of the disaster was Surgeon-Commander Sidney Hamilton (1912–2006). Before *Repulse* sank he had been treating the wounded. Then, after his rescue, he and the *Electra*'s doctor saved hundreds more injured men as the destroyer took survivors back to Singapore.

Captain Sir William Tennant of *Repulse*, pictured on board the *Vampire* after his rescue, chatting to another survivor, the battlecruiser's chaplain. In 1940, Tennant won acclaim for his masterful supervision of the evacuation from Dunkirk, a feat which earned him a knighthood, and the nickname 'Dunkirk Joe'. His handling of *Repulse* during the attack was equally exemplary.

The loss of Force Z was a body blow to the British Commonwealth, and marked a turning point in the defence of Malaya and Singapore. The end came on 15 February 1942, when Lieutenant-General Percival met the Japanese to negotiate the surrender of the city's beleaguered garrison.

radars and, above all, improved fire control radars, which would permit the laying down of dense barrages of flak in the path of the attacking aircraft. In an attack by torpedo bombers, it appeared that the close-range defensive capabilities of the lighter anti-aircraft guns were altogether far more effective. The 2-pounder 'pom-pom' was a weapon which was outdated and plagued by mechanical problems. Over the coming years, therefore, the Royal Navy would shift over to the use of lighter weapons – the 40mm Bofors and the 20mm Oerlikon. These, when supported by an efficient fire control system and deployed in large numbers, were the best available antidote to torpedo planes in the Royal Navy's arsenal.

While both sides learned lessons from the operation, there was also scope for an investigation of the commanders involved. After the event, Admiral Phillips was roundly criticised for not fully understanding the threat posed by naval air strikes against capital ships. He was certainly guilty of a lack of respect for naval air power. At a farewell dinner held in London before Phillips sailed, his RAF colleagues chided him about his refusal to admit that air power had a place in naval warfare. At the dinner, Air Commodore Arthur Harris, soon to become the head of Bomber Command, poked fun at the admiral, saying that when he found himself standing on a box on his bridge, and his flagship was under air attack, he would still deny that aircraft could damage his battleship. Instead, as Harris put it, 'Tom, when the first bomb hits, you'll say "My God – what a hell of a mine!" '

This attitude may well have influenced Phillips' decision to sortie from Singapore on 8 December. After all, the Japanese had already landed – their operation had achieved near-total surprise. All Force Z could achieve would be to disrupt the Japanese as they withdrew back to Indochina. With hindsight, some critics have pointed out that he should have called off the operation sooner, after he realised his force had been spotted by the Japanese on the evening of 9 December. Then again, he was impelled by the need to do something, partly to help those fighting on land in Malaya, but also for the honour of the navy. This was his one real chance to make a difference in the campaign, and he was understandably reluctant to call the operation off.

His diversion off Kuantan was also a dangerous gamble, as it meant his force would remain well within range of enemy land-based aircraft for much of the following day – 10 December. When he discovered the reports of a Japanese landing there were false, he still remained in the area, in the hope that the tug and barges he'd seen formed part of some larger Japanese amphibious force. Again, this is understandable – it was probably his last chance to alter the course of the campaign. The result, however, was that it placed Force Z firmly in harm's way that morning.

What is more unforgivable was his reluctance to call on air support during the previous evening. If Commonwealth fighter planes were there to protect Force Z that morning, off Kuantan, then they might well have been able to deter the Japanese, or at least inflict heavy losses on the unescorted bombers. It was Phillips' insistence on maintaining radio silence that prevented this, even though he knew the Japanese had sighted his ships the previous evening – the element of surprise he needed to succeed in his venture had already been lost.

For that matter, Rear-Admiral Matsunaga – the hero of the hour – can also be criticised. His last-minute change to his force might well have foiled his whole operation. By reducing the number of search aircraft he also reduced the probability of finding the British force. He also switched a squadron of the Mihoro *Kokutai* from torpedoes to bombs. His reasoning was that he wanted sufficient high-level bombers to be able to carry out simultaneous attacks from both high and low level. In effect, he simply diluted the effectiveness of his strike, as the high-level bombers achieved far less during the attack than the torpedo bombers did. Again, with hindsight it is clear that torpedo bombers were the decisive weapon in this attack, and would go on to be equally superior to high-level bombers in almost every other naval strike of the war. In the rear-admiral's defence, this superiority was not as clear in December 1941 as it would be during the months and years which followed.

Above all else, the sinking of Force Z demonstrated that the dominance the battleship had enjoyed in naval warfare had finally come to an abrupt end. For almost half a century, the battleship had reigned supreme as the arbiter of victory at sea. Throughout its life the torpedo had been a relatively ineffective weapon, and one which could be countered with relative ease, but which was now becoming increasingly effective when used by destroyers and submarines. Also, a new generation of aircraft had entered service which had the speed, capacity and agility to launch highly effective torpedo attacks. The torpedo bomber was a weapon that had finally come of age. What this battle demonstrated was that relatively cheap, mass-produced aircraft, if flown with skill and daring, and used in sufficient numbers, could prove more than a match for a hugely expensive battleship. So, 10 December 1941 marked a real historical milestone. In geopolitical terms, the sinking of Force Z signalled the imminent end for the British defence of Singapore – its surrender to the Japanese in turn marking the start of the disintegration of the British Empire. In the field of military and naval history, that date marked something of equally momentous importance. It was the day when the battleship ceased to be the dominant arbiter of naval power. In effect, 10 December 1941 marked the death of the battleship.

FURTHER READING

Ash, Bernard, *Someone had Blundered: The Story of the Repulse and the Prince of Wales* (Doubleday & Co.: London, 1961)

Bennet, H. G., *Why Singapore Fell* (Angus & Robertson: London, 1944)

Boyd, Andrew, *The Royal Navy in Eastern Waters* (Seaforth Publishing: Barnsley, 2017)

Campbell, John, *Naval Weapons of World War Two* (Conway Maritime Press: London, 1985)

Chippington, G., *Singapore: The Inexcusable Betrayal* (Self-Publishing Association: London, 1992)

Cull, Brian, *Buffaloes over Singapore: RAF, RAAF, RNZAF and Dutch Brewster Fighters in Action Over Malaya and the East Indies, 1941–1942* (Grub Street Press: London, 2008)

Dull, Paul S., *A Battle History of the Imperial Japanese Navy, 1941–1945* (Naval Institute Press: Annapolis, MD, 2007)

Friedman, Norman, *Naval Radar* (Conway Maritime Press: London, 1981)

Gardiner, Robert (ed.), *Conway's All the World's Fighting Ships, 1922–1946* (Conway Maritime Press: London, 1980)

Gardiner, Robert (ed.), *Conway's All the World's Fighting Ships, 1906–1921* (Conway Maritime Press: London, 1985)

Hough, Richard, *The Hunting of Force Z: Britain's Greatest Modern Naval Disaster* (Collins: London, 1963)

Japan Defence Agency – Research Section, National Defence Academy, *The Book of Military History: The Malayan Area* (Japanese Government Publication: Tokyo, 1969)

Jentschura, Hansgeorg, Dieter Jung and Peter Mickel, *Warships of the Imperial Japanese Navy, 1869–1945* (Arms & Armour Press: London, 1977)

Lewasor, James, *Singapore: The Battle that Changed the World* (Hodder & Stoughton: London, 1968)

Macdonald, Rod, *Force Z Shipwrecks of the South China Seas: HMS Repulse and HMS Prince of Wales* (Whittles Publishing: Dunbeath, 2013)

Middlebrook, Martin and Patrick Mahoney, *The Sinking of the Prince of Wales and Repulse: The End of the Battleship Era* (Leo Cooper: Barnsley, 2004); first published as *Battleship* (Allen Lane: London, 1977)

Okumiya, Masatake and Jiro Hirikoshi, *Zero! The Story of the Japanese Navy Air Force* (Cassell: London, 1957)

Parkes, Oscar, *British Battleships: A History of Design, Construction and Armament, 1860–1950* (Seeley Service Ltd: London, 1966)

Roskill, S. W., *The War at Sea*, vol. 1 (HM Stationery Office: London, 1954)

Stephen, Martin, *Sea Battles in Close-Up: World War 2* (Ian Allen Ltd: London, 1988)

Tarrant, V. E., *King George V Class Battleships* (Arms & Armour Press: London, 1991)

Whitley, M. J., *Battleships of World War Two: An International Encyclopedia* (Arms & Armour Press: London, 1998)

INDEX